move Up

Elementary
Student's Book

 B

Simon Greenall

Editorial Consultants

Bridget Green Mukogawa Fort Wright Institute
James Hunter Gonzaga University English Language Centre
Institute for Extended Learning, Community
Colleges of Spokane

MACMILLAN
HEINEMANN
English Language Teaching

Map of the Book

Lesson	Grammar and functions	Vocabulary	Skills and sounds
1 *Mystery* An extract from an article about Agatha Christie	Past simple (1): negatives *Wh-* questions	New words from a passage about Agatha Christie	**Reading:** predicting; reading for main ideas; reading for specific information **Writing:** writing a short autobiography **Speaking:** talking about your life
2 *Dates* Special occasions and important dates	Past simple (2): expressions of time	Ordinal numbers Dates, months of the year	**Sounds:** pronunciation of ordinal numbers and dates **Listening:** listening for main ideas; understanding text organization **Speaking:** talking about your answers to a quiz
3 *What's She Wearing?* Clothes and fashion	Describing people Present continuous or present simple	Items of clothing and accessories Colors Actions of the face, hand, and body	**Listening:** listening for specific information **Reading:** reading and answering a questionnaire **Speaking:** discussing your answers to the questionnaire
4 *I'm Going to Save Money* Talking about resolutions and future plans	*Going to* *Because* and *so*	New verbs from this lesson	**Reading:** predicting; reading for main ideas **Listening:** predicting; listening for main ideas **Writing:** writing resolutions; joining sentences with *because* and *so*
5 *Eating Out* Eating in different kinds of restaurants	*Would like* Talking about prices	Food items	**Listening:** predicting; listening for specific information **Sounds:** pronunciation of *like* and *'d like* **Reading:** reading for specific information **Speaking:** talking about eating out in your country
Progress Check *Lessons 1–5*	Review	Techniques for dealing with difficult words Word puzzle	**Sounds:** words with the same pronunciation but different spelling; /ʊ/ and /uː/; syllable stress; polite intonation **Writing:** preparing a quiz **Speaking:** asking and answering quiz questions
6 *May I Help You?* Shopping	Reflexive pronouns Saying what you want to buy Giving opinions Making decisions	Items of shopping	**Listening:** listening for specific information; listening for main ideas **Speaking:** talking about shopping habits
7 *Whose Bag Is This?* Describing objects and giving information	*Whose* Possessive pronouns Describing objects	Adjectives to describe objects Materials	**Speaking:** describing objects; acting out conversations in a Lost and Found Department **Listening:** listening for main ideas; listening for specific information
8 *What's the Problem?* Minor illnesses Medical care in the United States	Asking and saying how you feel Sympathizing *Should, shouldn't*	Adjectives to describe how you feel Nouns for illnesses Parts of the body	**Listening:** listening for main ideas **Reading:** reading for specific information; dealing with unfamiliar words **Writing:** writing a brochure about medical care for visitors to your country
9 *Country Factfile* Facts about Brazil, United States, and Sweden	Making comparisons (1): comparative and superlative forms of short adjectives	Adjectives to describe countries Measurements	**Sounds:** syllable stress **Reading:** reading for specific information **Listening:** listening for specific information **Writing:** writing a factfile for your country
10 *Olympic Spirit* Olympic sports	Making comparisons (2): comparative and superlative forms of longer adjectives	Sports Adjectives to describe sports	**Listening:** listening for main ideas **Speaking:** talking about Olympic sports and the Olympic games
Progress Check *Lessons 6–10*	Review	Adjectives and opposites Word Zigzag	**Sounds:** words which rhyme; /eɪ/ and /aɪ/; stress patterns **Speaking:** conversation building for sentences

Lesson	Grammar and functions	Vocabulary	Skills and sounds
11 *When in Rome, Do As the Romans Do* Customs and rules in different countries	Talking about obligation *Have to/don't have to/ should(n't)/can('t)*	New words from this lesson	**Reading:** reading for main ideas **Speaking:** talking about rules and customs in different countries **Listening:** listening for main ideas; listening for specific information **Writing:** writing advice and rules for visitors to your country
12 *Have You Ever Been to San Francisco?* Travel experiences	Present perfect (1): talking about experiences	New words from this lesson	**Reading:** reading for main ideas **Sounds:** strong and weak forms of *have* and *haven't* **Writing:** writing a postcard
13 *New York, New York!* Talking about New York	Present perfect (2): talking about unfinished events *For* and *since*	New words from this lesson	**Listening:** listening for main ideas; understanding text organisation **Speaking:** predicting; talking about experiences **Writing:** writing a paragraph about your partner
14 *Planning the Perfect Day* Favorite outings	Imperatives Infinitive of purpose	Words connected with outings	**Speaking:** talking about a perfect day **Reading:** reading for main ideas **Writing:** writing advice for planning the perfect day out
15 *She Sings Well* Schooldays	Adverbs	Adverbs and their opposites	**Sounds:** identifying attitude and mood **Reading:** reading for main ideas; reading for specific information **Listening:** listening for main ideas **Speaking:** talking about achievement at school
Progress Check Lessons 11–15	Review	Collocation	**Sounds:** words with the same vowel sound; /əʊ/ and /ɔː/; word stress and a change of meaning **Reading:** reading for specific information; focusing on unnecessary words
16 *Cruisin'!* Travel by ship and plane	Future simple (1): (*will*) for decisions	Words connected with travel by ship and plane	**Listening:** listening for specific information **Reading:** reading for specific information **Speaking:** acting out a role play in a travel agency
17 *What Will It Be Like in the Future?* Talking about the future	Future simple (2): (*will*) for predictions	Nouns and adjectives for the weather	**Listening:** listening for specific information **Reading:** predicting; reading for specific information **Speaking:** making predictions about the future
18 *Hamlet Was Written by Shakespeare* World facts	Active and passive	Verbs used for passive	**Speaking:** talking about true and false sentences **Reading:** reading and answering a quiz **Listening:** listening for specific information **Writing:** writing a quiz about your country
19 *She Said It Wasn't Far* Staying in a youth hostel	Reported speech: statements	Items connected with travel	**Reading:** reading for main ideas; reading for specific information **Listening:** listening for specific information **Writing:** writing a letter of complaint
20 *Dear Jan... Love Ruth* A short story by Nick McIver	Tense review	New words from this lesson	**Reading:** predicting; reading for main ideas **Listening:** listening for specific information **Writing:** writing a different ending to the story
Progress Check Lessons 16–20	Review	Prepositions Word association	**Sounds:** /ɔː/ and /ɔɪ/; syllable stress **Speaking:** playing *Move Up Snakes and Ladders*

Past simple (1): negatives; *wh-* questions

Agatha Christie was the most successful writer of detective stories of all time. People all over the world read her stories of Hercule Poirot and Miss Marple. But when she died in 1976 there was a final mystery: why did she disappear for eleven days in December 1926?

Agatha Christie was born in September 1890. She lived with her family in Devon, England. In 1914 she married Colonel Archibald Christie. She wrote her first detective story in 1920 and soon she was very successful.

But Agatha Christie didn't have a happy marriage. On a cold night in December 1926 she left home in her car. The following morning, the police found the empty car, but there was no sign of Agatha Christie. Two days later, they told the newspapers that they didn't know where she was. Everyone thought she was dead.

But 250 miles away in Yorkshire, a waiter in a hotel saw a guest who looked like Agatha Christie, and he told the police. Eleven days after her disappearance, her husband found her again in the hotel dining room.

The couple were soon divorced. She married Sir Max Mallowan, an archaeologist, in 1930 and she continued to write her mysteries. But she didn't explain what happened in 1926. Did she want to kill herself? Did she want to show her husband that she didn't love him? Did she hope to sell more books?

Over the years, Agatha Christie wrote more than 80 mysteries and sold over 300 million books. But she didn't tell anyone why she disappeared in December 1926.

Why did Agatha Christie disappear?

PENGUIN BOOKS

MYSTERY AND CRIME

MURDER ON THE ORIENT EXPRESS

AGATHA CHRISTIE

116

VOCABULARY AND READING

1. Work in pairs. You're going to read an article about Agatha Christie. Do you know who she was? Talk about anything you know about her. Think about what you'd like to find out about her.

2. Work in pairs. Look at the title of the article and the words in the box. What do you think happened?

successful writer detective story mystery marriage unhappy left home disappear waiter hotel guest husband find divorced kill tell

3. Read the article and choose the correct answer to the question under the photograph.

1. Because she was unhappy.
2. We don't know.
3. Because she wanted to kill herself.

Did you guess correctly in 2?

4. Put a check (✓) by the statements which are true.

1. Agatha Christie married when she was fifteen.
2. The police found her in the car.
3. The police said that she was dead.
4. A hotel waiter recognized her.
5. Her husband found her at home.
6. She married a crime writer.
7. She wrote over eighty detective stories.
8. She died at the age of seventy-six.

5. Work in pairs.

Student A: Turn to Communication Activity 4 on page 51.

Student B: Turn to Communication Activity 8 on page 52.

GRAMMAR

Past simple (1): negatives **You form the negative for all verbs except** *be* **with** *didn't* **+ infinitive without** *to.* *She **didn't have** a happy marriage.*   *She **didn't explain** her disappearance.* *Wh-* questions **You form** *Wh-* **questions for all verbs except** *be* **with a** *Wh-* **question word** **(*who, what, when, why*)** **+** *did* **+ infinitive without** *to.* ***What did** Agatha Christie **do?**   **Why did** she **disappear?** *Where **was** she born?*

1. Correct the false statements in *Vocabulary and Reading* activity 4.

She didn't marry when she was fifteen. She married when she was twenty-four.

2. Here are some answers about Agatha Christie. Write the questions. Use *wh-* question words.

1. She wrote detective stories.
2. In September 1890.
3. In Devon.
4. Colonel Archibald Christie.
5. In December 1926.
6. In a hotel in Yorkshire.
7. Eleven days after her disappearance.
8. He was an archaeologist.

3. Turn to Communication Activity 3 on page 51.

WRITING AND SPEAKING

1. Write a short autobiography. Say:

– where you were born   – when you started school
– where you lived   – if there were any special events in your life

I was born in 1982. I lived with my family in Vitoria. Then we moved to São Paulo.

2. Work in pairs and exchange your autobiographies. Write extra questions about your partner's autobiography.

How long did you live in Vitoria? When did you move to São Paulo?

3. Read your partner's questions. Rewrite your autobiography and include the answers.

I was born in 1982 in Vitoria, and I lived there with my family for ten years. Then we moved to São Paulo in...

2 Dates

Past simple (2): expressions of time

VOCABULARY AND SOUNDS

1. Match the words in the box with the numbers below.

> eighth eleventh fifth first fourth ninth second
> seventh sixth tenth third twelfth

1st 2nd 3rd 4th 5th 6th 7th 8th 9th 10th
11th 12th

1st – first

2. Write the words for the following numbers.

13th 17th 20th 21st 22nd 23rd 27th 30th 31st

13th – thirteenth

3. Notice how:

– you write
March 1   April 13

– you say
March first   April thirteenth

▭ Now listen and repeat these dates.

March 1   April 13   September 23   January 4
July 30   May 2   June 20   October 10

4. Work in pairs. What dates are the following?

New Year's Day   your birthday
the national day or an important day in
your country   yesterday   today

| January February March April May June July |
| August September October November December |

New Year's Day is January first.

LISTENING AND SPEAKING

1. Match these words with the special days below.

present   church   letter   party   reception
driver's license   certificate   card   forget   ring

☐ an important birthday   ☐ a wedding day
☐ passing an exam   ☐ an anniversary
☐ Independence Day

2. 🔲 You're going to hear three people talking about one of the special days. Listen and put the number of the speaker by the special day he/she is describing in 1.

3. Work in pairs and check your answers to 2. Which speaker uses the following expressions?

last Thursday   yesterday evening   five months ago
in 1987   in August   from nine to five
on December eleventh   at the end of the year

🔲 Listen again and check.

GRAMMAR

Past simple (2): expressions of time
You can use these expresssions of past time to say when something happened.
last   *night/Thursday/August/month/year*
I saw him last year.

in   *August/1987*
We got married in 1987.

ago   *days/weeks/months ago*
We went on vacation three weeks ago.

yesterday   *morning/afternoon/evening*
I met her yesterday morning.

at the end of   *the day/month/year*
My birthday is at the end of the month.

on   *Monday/December eleventh*
My birthday is on December eleventh.

1. Complete the sentences with an expression of time in the grammar box.

1. I went to the dentist _____.
2. I did my homework _____.
3. I started studying English _____.
4. I bought someone a present _____.
5. I met my best friend _____.
6. I wrote a postcard _____.

2. Work in pairs. Ask and answer the questions.

1. When did you last buy a new coat?
2. When did you get home yesterday?
3. When did you last go to a movie?
4. When did you get up this morning?
5. When did you last have a birthday?
6. When did you start this lesson?

1. A year ago.

SPEAKING

1. Work in pairs and answer the questions in the quiz. You score 2 points if you get the right answer, and 1 point if it's very close. Your teacher will decide.

When did...

1. ... the Berlin Wall come down?
2. ... the Russian Revolution start?
3. ... astronauts first land on the moon?
4. ... the first atom bomb explode?
5. ... Columbus discover America?
6. ... the Chinese build the Great Wall?
7. ... the Second World War start?
8. ... John F. Kennedy die?
9. ... the First World War start?
10. ... you start studying English?

2. Work in two pairs and continue the quiz in 1.
Pair A: Turn to Communication Activity 2 on page 51.
Pair B: Turn to Communication Activity 13 on page 53.

5

What's She Wearing?

Describing people; present continuous or present simple

VOCABULARY AND LISTENING

1. Look at the people in the pictures and say what they're wearing. Use the words in the box to help you.

> pants jeans skirt socks shorts dress tie shirt
> T-shirt jacket sweater shoes sneakers

Turn to Communication Activity 7 on page 51 to find out what the other words are.

2. Which words can you use to describe the clothes:

– you're wearing right now?   – you usually wear?

> comfortable fashionable casual formal warm

3. Look at the pictures again and use these words to describe the people.

> sit down stand smile laugh wear

4. 📼 Listen to Jan and find out who the people in the pictures are.

5. Work in pairs and check your answers. Then complete the chart with as much detail as possible.

📼 Listen again and check.

	Erin	John	Ed	Louise
What's he/she wearing?				
What's he/she doing?				

FUNCTIONS AND GRAMMAR

Describing people

She's wearing a black dress.　　*She's sitting down.*
She's smiling.
He's the man sitting down in the armchair.

Present continuous or present simple
You use the present continuous to say what is happening now or around now.
*She's **wearing** a skirt.*　　*He's **living** in Hawaii right now.*
You use the present simple to describe something which is true for a long time.
*She usually **wears** jeans.*　　*He **lives** in New York.*

1. Choose the correct verb form.

1. He usually *wears/is wearing* a suit.
2. She *smiles/is smiling* at him.
3. Greg *is standing/stands* by the door.
4. Maria is the person who *is talking/talks* to Ken.
5. Where *are you working/do you work* right now?
6. You usually *stand up/are standing up* when you meet someone.
7. Ricardo *smokes/is smoking*, but he *doesn't smoke/isn't smoking* now.
8. Alfonso *wears/is wearing* brown shoes every day.

2. Work in pairs.

Student A: Choose someone in the class and describe him/her. Don't say who he/she is.

Student B: Listen to Student A's description of someone in the class. Can you guess who it is?

He's wearing jeans.
He's sitting down.

3. Write full answers to the questions in the chart in *Vocabulary and Listening* activity 5.

Erin's wearing jeans and a T-shirt. She's standing by the door.

READING AND SPEAKING

1. Read the questionnaire and answer the questions.

What do your clothes say about you?

1. You see someone with blue hair wearing a yellow jacket and red pants. What do you do?
a. smile　b. laugh　c. wear the same clothes

2. You are going to an interview. What do you wear?
a. jeans　b. a suit　c. something comfortable

3. You're going to work. What do you wear?
a. pants　b. sneakers　c. a jacket

4. You're going to a party. What do you wear?
a. a jacket　b. a T-shirt　c. a suit/dress

5. You're buying a new jacket. What color do you buy?
a. black　b. red　c. orange

6. You're buying clothes for cold weather. Which is more important?
a. comfort　b. warmth　c. fashion

7. You want to give a good impression. Which style do you choose?
a. comfortable but fashionable
b. fashionable and formal　c. casual

8. What kind of clothes do you prefer?
a. cheap　b. expensive　c. fashionable

9. You're talking to someone who is wearing a very ugly suit. What do you do?
a. say you hate it　b. say nothing
c. say you love it

10. It's a very hot day in the park. What do you wear?
a. a suit　b. pants and a sweater
c. shorts and a T-shirt

2. Work in pairs and talk about your answers to the questionnaire.

3. Turn to Communication Activity 15 on page 53 and find out what your clothes say about you.

4 *I'm Going to Save Money*

Going to; because* and *so

READING AND LISTENING

1. Read the passage *My New Year's Resolution*.
Who do you think you can see in the pictures?

My New Year's Resolution...

1. "I'm going to see my friends more often." *Phil*
2. "I'm going to save money." *Andrea*
3. "I'm going to change my job." *Pete*
4. "We're going to travel around Europe."
   Andrew and Mary
5. "We're going to take Spanish lessons." *Jill and Steve*
6. "I'm going to spend more time with my parents." *Jenny*
7. "We're going to invite more friends for dinner."
   Henry and June
8. "I'm going to get in shape." *Kate*
9. "I'm not going to take work home." *Dave*
10. "We're going to move." *Judy and Frank*

2. Match the resolutions in 1 with the reasons below.

a. We don't speak any foreign languages.

b. We don't entertain very much.

c. I hate my work.

d. I stay at home all the time.

e. Our grandparents came from there.

f. Our house is too small.

g. I never see my family.

h. I want to spend more time with my children.

i. I spend too much.

j. I don't do enough exercise.

3. 🔲 Listen to four people talking about their resolutions and the reasons. Find out who's speaking. Did you guess correctly in 2?

4. Work in pairs. Can you remember any other details about what the speakers said?

🔲 Now listen again and check.

GRAMMAR

> *Going to*
>
> **You use *going to* + infinitive:**
> **– to talk about future intentions or plans.**
> *I'm going to see my friends more often.*
> *I'm not going to take work home.*
> **– to talk about something which we can see now is**
> **sure to happen in the future.**
> *I'm going to have a baby.*
>
> *Because* and *so*
> **You can join two sentences with *because* to describe**
> **a reason.**
> *Judy and Frank are going to move **because** their house is*
> *too small.*
> **You can join the same two sentences with *so* to**
> **describe a consequence.**
> *Judy and Frank's house is too small, **so** they're going to move.*

1. Look at these sentences and explain the difference
between them.

I go to work at nine o'clock.

I'm going to work at nine o'clock.

2. Work in pairs. Check your answers to *Reading and Listening* activity 3. Say what the speakers are going to/not going to do.

Henry and June are going to invite more friends for dinner.

3. Work in pairs. Say what you're going to do this weekend. Here are some ideas:

get up late   do some housework   play football
go out for a meal   read a newspaper
meet some friends   watch TV   go for a walk

4. Choose three sentences in *Reading and Listening* activities 1 and 2 and join them with *because*.

Andrea is going to save money because she spends too much.

5. Choose three more sentences in *Reading and Listening* activities 1 and 2 and join them with *so*.

Kate doesn't do enough exercise, so she's going to get in shape.

VOCABULARY AND WRITING

1. Here are some verbs from this lesson. Can you remember which nouns or noun-phrases they went with in *My New Year's Resolution*?

save take spend get invite change

save money...

2. Write what you're going to do before you finish *Move Up* Elementary.

I'm going to save more money.

3. Write why you're going to do the things you wrote in 2.

I want to take a long vacation.

4. Join the sentences you wrote in 2 with the sentences you wrote in 3 using *because*.

I'm going to save more money because I want to take a long vacation.

Eating Out

***Would like*; talking about prices**

VOCABULARY AND LISTENING

1. Look at the words in the box. Which pictures of food and drink can you see on the menu?

> cheeseburger soda French fries ice cream sandwich salad
> pizza apple pie cheesecake hot dog spaghetti juice steak
> Jello coffee mayonnaise strawberry

2. Which word doesn't belong?

1. cheeseburger soda juice coffee
2. apple pie cheesecake ice cream spaghetti
3. pizza strawberry steak hot dog
4. French fries Jello salad mayonnaise

3. Look at this conversation in a fast food restaurant. Decide where the sentences a–f go in the conversation.

CASHIER	Good afternoon. May I help you?
CUSTOMER	(1) _____
CASHIER	Would you like a regular or a large soda?
CUSTOMER	(2) _____.
CASHIER	Would you like anything else?
CUSTOMER	(3) _____
CASHIER	What flavor would you like?
CUSTOMER	(4) _____
CASHIER	OK.
CUSTOMER	(5) _____
CASHIER	That's six dollars and forty-nine cents, please.
CUSTOMER	(6) _____
CASHIER	Thank you.

a. Regular.
b. Good afternoon. Yes, I'd like a cheeseburger with fries and an orange soda.
c. Strawberry, please.
d. How much is that?
e. Yes, I'd like some ice cream, please.
f. Here you are.

4. 🔊 Listen and check your answers to 3.

FUNCTIONS

> *Would like*
>
> **You use *would like* + infinitive/noun to ask for something politely.**
> *I'd like a cheeseburger and an orange soda, please.*
> ***Would you like** a regular or a large soda?*
> *I'd like some ice cream, please.*
> *What flavor **would you like?***
>
> **Remember**
> **– you use *like* to say what you like all the time.**
> *I **like** orange soda.* (= always)
> **– you use *would like* to say what you want now.**
> *I'd **like** an orange soda.* (= now)
>
> **Talking about prices**
> *How much is it?   Two dollars and ninety-nine cents.*

1. Choose the correct answer.

1. Would you like a drink?
   a. No, I don't like a drink.   b. No, thank you.
2. What would you like to eat?
   a. I'd like a pizza.   b. I like pizza.
3. Would you like some coffee?
   a. Yes, please.   b. No, I don't.
4. Do you like spaghetti?
   a. Yes, please.   b. Yes.
5. May I help you?
   a. No, you don't.   b. Yes, I'd like a burger.
6. Would you like to order?
   a. Yes, a cheeseburger, please.
   b. Yes, I like cheeseburgers.

2. Work in pairs and act out the conversation in *Vocabulary and Listening* activity 3. Choose other items from the menu.

3. Work in pairs. Look at the menu and ask and say how much things cost.

SOUNDS

🔲   Listen and check (✓) the sentences you hear.

1. a. I like beer.   b. I'd like a beer.
2. a. He likes ice cream.   b. He'd like ice cream.
3. a. We like the check.   b. We'd like the check.
4. a. I like pizza.   b. I'd like pizza.
5. a. She'd like a salad.   b. She likes a salad.
6. a. Would you like Jello?   b. Do you like Jello?

READING AND SPEAKING

1. You're going to read a passage about eating out in the United States. First, check you know what the underlined words in the passage mean.

2. Read *Eating Out in the U.S.A.* and find out what it says about:

– types of restaurants   – where to sit   – who to pay
– how much to tip   – other advice

EATING OUT IN THE U.S.A.

In the United States, there are many types of restaurant. Fast food restaurants are very famous, with McDonalds and Kentucky Fried Chicken in many countries around the world. You look at a <u>menu</u> above the <u>counter</u>, and say what you'd like to eat. You pay the person who serves you. You take your food and sit down or take it out. When you finish your meal, you put the <u>empty container</u> and paper in the <u>trash can</u>. There's no need to leave a tip.

In a coffee shop you sit at the counter or at a table. You don't wait for the <u>waitress</u> to show you where to sit. She usually brings you coffee when you sit down. You tell her what you'd like to eat and she brings it to you. You pay the <u>cashier</u> as you leave. A diner is like a coffee shop but usually has a long counter and <u>booths</u> to sit at.

In a family restaurant the atmosphere is casual, but the waiter shows you where to sit. Often the waiter tells you his name, but you don't need to tell him yours. If you don't eat everything, your waiter gives you a <u>doggy bag</u> to take your food home. You <u>add</u> an extra fifteen per cent to the <u>check</u> as a tip.

In top class restaurants, you need a reservation and you need to arrive on time. The waiter shows you where to sit. If you have wine, he may ask you to <u>taste</u> it. You can only <u>refuse</u> it if it tastes bad, not if you don't like it. When you get your check, add it up, and then add fifteen to twenty per cent to it as a tip. You pay the waiter.

3. Work in pairs and check your answers. Compare eating out in the U.S.A. with eating out in your country.

VOCABULARY

1. When you see a word you don't understand, stop and ask yourself these questions:

– what part of speech is it?
– can I guess what it means?
– can the rest of the passage help me understand it?

Try not to use a dictionary or ask your teacher every time.

Look at this extract from the passage in Lesson 5. Some of the difficult words are missing. Think about your answers to the questions above. Don't try to remember the exact word.

In the United States, there are many types of restaurant. Fast food restaurants are very famous, with McDonalds and Kentucky Fried Chicken in many countries around the world. You look at a _____ above the _____, and say what you'd like to eat. You pay the person who serves you. You take your food and sit down or take it out. When you finish your meal, you put the _____ container and paper in the _____. There's no need to leave a tip.

In a coffee shop you sit at the counter or at a table. You don't wait for the _____ to show you where to sit. She usually brings you coffee when you sit down. You pay the _____ as you leave. A diner is like a coffee shop but usually has a long counter and _____ to sit at.

Now look back at page 11 to find out what the missing words are.

2. Find ten words in the word puzzle. They go in two directions (↓) and (→). Five words are to do with food and drink and five words are to do with clothes.

c	s	o	c	k	a	s	c	v	g
h	a	m	b	u	r	g	e	r	a
o	s	d	f	g	t	k	l	m	j
c	h	e	e	s	e	c	a	k	e
o	d	f	v	a	e	z	p	s	a
l	c	x	e	l	s	f	p	h	n
a	f	w	q	a	h	v	l	i	s
t	r	y	u	d	o	n	e	r	e
e	t	h	h	t	e	m	u	t	q
t	d	r	e	s	s	k	r	h	x

3. Choose one of the other topics in Lessons 1 to 5 and make a word puzzle.

When you're ready, work in pairs and do each other's word puzzles.

GRAMMAR

1. Complete the sentences with *ago, from, to, last, yesterday, in, at.*

1. He started work _____ morning.
2. We went camping _____ summer.
3. I started studying French _____ year.
4. He called me five minutes _____.
5. It was open _____ nine _____ five.
6. He left _____ the end of the week.

2. Choose the correct verb form.

1. I *wear/am wearing* jeans most of the time.
2. He's the man who *stands/is standing* next to Jim.
3. He *smokes/is smoking* twenty cigarettes a day.
4. I always *shake/am shaking* hands when I meet someone.
5. She *smiles/is smiling* at him right now.
6. I *speak/am speaking* fluent English.

1. I wear jeans most of the time.

3. Write five things which you're going to do next month.

I'm going to visit my sister next month.

4. Join the two sentences by rewriting them with *because*.

1. I'm hungry. I'd like something to eat.
2. We don't have any pizza. Would you like spaghetti?
3. I like him. I'm going to see Tom Cruise's new film.
4. I'm going to live in New York. I like the people there.
5. He can't see. He doesn't have his glasses.
6. We went on vacation last year. We're not going away this year.

1. I'd like something to eat because I'm hungry.

5. Rewrite the sentences in 4 with *so*.

1. I'm hungry so I'd like something to eat.

SOUNDS

1. 🔲 Listen and repeat the following words.

meet   their   know   sea   son   write   eye   right   no   sun   for   there   I   four   knows   too   see   meat   nose   two

Write the pairs of words which sound the same but have different spelling.

meet – meat

2. Say these words out loud. Is the underlined sound /ʊ/ or /uː/?

f<u>oo</u>d   sh<u>oe</u>   y<u>ou</u>   g<u>oo</u>d   s<u>ou</u>p   c<u>oo</u>k   b<u>oo</u>k   d<u>o</u>   f<u>oo</u>t   c<u>oo</u>l   p<u>u</u>t   j<u>ui</u>ce   b<u>oo</u>t

🔲 Now listen and check. As you listen, say the words out loud.

3. Look at these words. Underline the stressed syllable.

banana   cabbage   potato   bacon   casual   sneakers   cashier   cheesecake   salad   hamburger   toothpaste

🔲 Listen and check. As you listen, say the words out loud.

4. 🔲 Listen to these questions. Put a check (✓) if you think the speaker sounds polite.

1. Can I help you?
2. What would you like to eat?
3. Would you like a drink?
4. Would you like anything else?

Now say the questions out loud. Try to sound polite.

WRITING AND SPEAKING

1. Work in groups of three or four. You're going to prepare a quiz about important historical facts.
Write at least ten questions about important events/people in history. Think about:

– life and death of famous people
– inventions and discoveries
– wars
– political events
– artistic creations

2. Work with another group. In turn, ask and answer questions from your quizzes. You score one point for each correct answer. The group with the most points is the winner.

May I Help You?

Reflexive pronouns; saying what you want to buy; giving opinions; making decisions

SPEAKING AND LISTENING

1. Match the sentences 1–4 with the sentences a–d to make four conversations.

1. Can I carry that for you?
2. Did you make it?
3. Are you buying this for yourself?
4. They bought themselves a new one.

a. No, it's for a friend.
b. Did they? What kind?
c. No, Billy made it himself.
d. No, it's OK. I can carry it myself.

2. Work in pairs and check your answers to 1. Choose one conversation and write two or three sentences before and after it. Act out your conversation to the rest of the class.

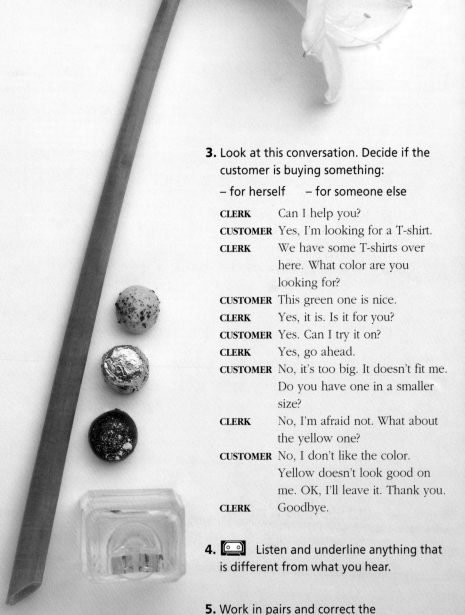

3. Look at this conversation. Decide if the customer is buying something:

– for herself   – for someone else

CLERK	Can I help you?
CUSTOMER	Yes, I'm looking for a T-shirt.
CLERK	We have some T-shirts over here. What color are you looking for?
CUSTOMER	This green one is nice.
CLERK	Yes, it is. Is it for you?
CUSTOMER	Yes. Can I try it on?
CLERK	Yes, go ahead.
CUSTOMER	No, it's too big. It doesn't fit me. Do you have one in a smaller size?
CLERK	No, I'm afraid not. What about the yellow one?
CUSTOMER	No, I don't like the color. Yellow doesn't look good on me. OK, I'll leave it. Thank you.
CLERK	Goodbye.

4. 🔲 Listen and underline anything that is different from what you hear.

5. Work in pairs and correct the conversation.

GRAMMAR AND FUNCTIONS

> **Reflexive pronouns**
> **You usually use a reflexive pronoun when the subject and the object of a sentence are the same.**
>
> *myself yourself himself herself itself ourselves yourselves themselves*
> *I enjoyed* **myself.**
>
> **Saying what you want to buy**   **Giving opinions**
> *I'd like a…*   *It's too big/small/long/short.*
> *I'm looking for…*   *It doesn't look good on me.*
> *Can I try it on?*   *It doesn't fit me.*
> *Do you have a/any…?*   *I don't like the color.*
> *Do you have it in another color?*
>
> **Making decisions**
> *Can I try it in a different size?*
> *I'll have this/these.*   *I'll take it/them.*   *I'll leave it.*

1. Complete the sentences with a reflexive pronoun.

1. Was that T-shirt a gift? No, I bought it for _____.
2. Tim and I enjoyed _____ at the disco last night.
3. She doesn't live by _____ . She lives with friends.
4. Can I have some coffee? Yes, would you like to serve _____?
5. They taught _____ to speak Russian. They didn't take lessons.
6. He's unhealthy and smokes too much. He doesn't take care of _____.

2. Work in pairs and act out the conversation in *Speaking and Listening* activity 3.

VOCABULARY AND SPEAKING

1. Look at the words in the box. Which things can you see in the picture?

> chocolate   cookies   cakes   flowers   milk   perfume   jeans   soap

2. Which words in 1 do the words below go with?

> box   package   bottle   bunch   pair   bar

a box of chocolate …

3. Work in pairs. Which things do you buy for yourself? Which things do you buy as gifts for other people?

I often buy chocolate for myself.

4. Work in pairs.

Student A: You're a store clerk. You sell the things in the picture.
Student B: You're a customer. You want to buy something in the picture.

Act out a conversation.

SPEAKING

1. Work in groups of three or four and discuss your answers to the questions.

1. Do you like shopping?
2. When you go shopping, do you usually go by yourself?
3. Do you know what you want to buy?
4. Do you usually buy things for yourself?
5. How often do you buy things for other people?
6. Who do you buy gifts for?
7. When do you give gifts?
8. What do you buy for gifts?

2. Find out what other students' answers are.

3. Report back to your group.

Ibrahim often buys things for himself.

Whose Bag Is This?

Whose; possessive pronouns; describing objects

VOCABULARY AND SPEAKING

1. Complete the sentences below the pictures with words from the box.

> short   long   square   round   small   large   rectangular
> heavy   light

2. Say what the things in the pictures are made of. Use the words in the box.

> glass   leather   metal   plastic   paper   wood

The ruler is made of plastic.

3. Work in pairs. Choose an object in the classroom. In turn, ask and answer questions to try to guess the object your partner is describing.

A *It's square.*
B *Is it a book?*
A *No. It's made of glass.*
B *Is it the window?*
A *Yes.*

4. Match the conversations and the pictures below.

A Excuse me, is this yours?   **A** Whose is this?
B No, it isn't mine. It's his.   **B** It's theirs.

a. *It's long.*
b. *It's short.*
c. *It's square.*
d. *It's _____.*
e. *It's _____.*
f. *It's _____.*
g. *It's _____.*
h. *It's _____.*
i. *It's _____.*

16

GRAMMAR AND FUNCTIONS

Whose
You use *whose* to ask who something belongs to.
Whose bag is this?
Whose shoes are these?

Possessive pronouns
You use possessive pronouns to say who something belongs to.
mine   yours   his   hers   ours   theirs
*Whose bag is this?   It's **mine.***
*Whose shoes are these?   They're **his.***

Describing objects
You don't usually put more than two or three adjectives together.
What's it like?
It's a small, plastic ruler.

1. Look at these possessive adjectives.

my   your   his   her   its   our   their

Which letter do you add to the possessive adjective to make a possessive pronoun? Which possessive pronouns are the exception?

2. Choose the correct word in these sentences.

1. Whose is this? It's *my/mine*.
2. Where did I put *my/mine* bag?
3. These aren't *her/hers* shoes. They're *my/mine*.
4. *Whose/who's* that woman?
5. Are these *their/theirs* books? No, they're *our/ours*.
6. *Whose/who's* coat is this?

3. Work in groups of four or five. Put two personal possessions on a desk or in a bag. Go around, in turn, holding up or taking out a possession, asking and saying who it belongs to.

A Whose is this?
B It's mine. And whose is this?
C It's his.

LISTENING AND SPEAKING

1. You're going to hear a conversation in a Lost and Found Department. Look at the form below. Match 1–9 and the questions a–i.

Lost and Found	
1. Name	Ms. Joan Fairfield
2. Address	10510 N Nevada, Springfield, Illinois 92703
3. Telephone	509 555-6463
4. Lost article	a purse
5. Date of loss	July 20
6. Time of loss	10 A.M.
7. Place of loss	Disneyland – in Fantasyland
8. Description	small, square, and it was made of black leather
9. Contents	a purse, a calculator, an address book, a comb

a. What did you lose?
b. Where did you lose it?
c. What was in it?
d. What date did you lose it?
e. What's your name?
f. What's your address?
g. What's it like?
h. What's your telephone number?
i. What time did you lose it?

2. 📼 Look at the Lost and Found form. Listen and underline any information which is different from what you hear.

3. Work in pairs. Correct any information which was different.
📼 Listen again and check.

4. Work in pairs. Act out the conversation you heard in 2. Use the form and the questions to help you.

What's the Problem?

Asking and saying how you feel; sympathising; *should, shouldn't*

VOCABULARY AND LISTENING

1. Look at the words in the box. Find:

– two types of medicine
– six medical problems or illnesses
– four adjectives to describe how you feel
– seven parts of the body

> arm aspirin back cold (noun)
> cough cough medicine dizzy
> faint finger foot hand
> headache leg sick
> sore throat stomachache
> temperature tired toe

2. 🔊 Listen to three conversations. Say what's wrong with each person.

The first person has a headache.

3. Put the number of the person by what you think he/she should do.

☐ go to bed
☐ stay home
☐ drink lots of water
☐ stop smoking
☐ get some exercise
☐ go to the doctor
☐ keep warm
☐ eat nothing for 24 hours
☐ lie down

FUNCTIONS AND GRAMMAR

> **Asking and saying how you feel**
> *What's the problem?*   *I don't feel very well.*
> *What's the matter?*   *I feel sick.*
> *Are you all right?*   *I have a headache.*
>   *My back hurts.*
>
> **Sympathizing**
> *Oh dear!*   *Too bad!*   *Oh, I'm sorry to hear that.*
>
> ***Should, shouldn't***
> ***Should* and *shouldn't* are modal verbs.**
> **You use *should* and *shouldn't* to give advice.**
> *You **should** go to bed.*   (= It's a good idea to go to bed).
> *You **shouldn't** go to work.*   (= It's a bad idea to go to work).
> **(For more information about modal verbs, see Grammar Review page 58.)**

1. Look at the functions and grammar box and answer the questions.

1. What follows *I feel* – an adjective or a noun?
2. What follows *I have* – an adjective or a noun?
3. What comes before *hurts* a person or a part of the body?

2. Work in pairs and say what the people in the conversations in *Vocabulary and Listening* activity 2 should or shouldn't do.

I think he should go to bed.
He shouldn't go to work.

3. Work in pairs.

Student A: Turn to Communication Activity 6 on page 51.
Student B: Turn to Communication Activity 9 on page 52.

READING AND WRITING

1. Read and answer the questions for your country.

1. When you're sick, do you go to a specialist who knows about your illness or to your family doctor?
2. Are there both men and women doctors?
3. Where do you get medicine in your country?
4. Do you ever go to the doctor if you're feeling fine?
5. Do doctors visit you at home?
6. What do you do in an emergency?
7. Do friends and relatives visit you in the hospital?
8. Do you pay for medical treatment?

The Nation's Health

In the United States, when you're sick, you go to a doctor near your home. Doctors are men and women, and you can say which you prefer. You usually only spend about ten minutes with the doctor. They can usually say what the problem is very quickly, and often give you a prescription for some medicine. You get this at the drugstore. If not, they may suggest you go to a specialist.

Most people only go to their doctor when they're sick. People with colds and coughs don't go to their doctor but to the drugstore, to buy medicine. In an emergency you can call 911 for an ambulance. The ambulance takes you to the hospital for treatment. Friends and relatives visit you in hospital at certain hours of the day, but they don't stay there.

You have to pay for a visit to the doctor or to the hospital in the United States, and for the medicines that doctors prescribe for you. Most people have medical insurance to cover these costs.

2. Read the brochure *The Nation's Health* and find the answers to the questions in 1 for the United States.

3. Work in pairs. Is medical care in your country different from in the United States?

4. Prepare a brochure about medical care for a foreign visitor to your country. Write answers to the questions in 1. Use the passage to help you.

When you're sick in Japan you should go to a specialist…

9 *Country Factfile*

Making comparisons (1): comparative and superlative forms of short adjectives

VOCABULARY AND SOUNDS

1. Match the adjectives with their opposites in the box.

> big cold dry fast high hot low old
> slow small wet young

2. Which of the words for measurements in the box do you use to describe the following?

– area – length – temperature

> Fahrenheit yard foot inch
> mile square mile

3. 🔲 Listen to the following words used to talk about countries and underline the stressed syllable.

> area average temperature rainfall
> population education

Now say the words out loud.

4. Match the words for measurements in the box in 2 with their abbreviations below.

in. ft. yd.· °F sq. mi. mi.

READING AND LISTENING

1. Look at the country factfile and decide if these statements are true or false.

1. The United States is smaller than Brazil.
2. It's colder in Brazil than in the United States.
3. It's drier in Brazil than in the United States.
4. The population in the United States is smaller than in Brazil.
5. The Brazilian armed services are smaller than the American armed services.
6. Brazilian children are younger when they start school than American children.
7. Brazilian children are older when they can leave school than American children.

Country Factfile

	Brazil	United States	Sweden
1. Land area	3,286,488 sq. mi.	3,732,396 sq. mi.	
2. Average temperature	Rio de Janeiro January 79°F July 69°F	Washington D.C. January 35°F July 80°F	
3. Rainfall	Rio de Janeiro 43 in.	Washington D.C. 39 in.	
4. Population	(1995) 161,382,000	(1995) 263,437,000	
5. Armed Services	296,700 troops	1,704,000 troops	
6. Education	Free and compulsory for all children between 7 and 14	Free and compulsory for all children between 6 and 16	

2. 🔊 You're going to hear Karl answering questions about Sweden. Listen and put the letter corresponding to the correct answer in the Country Factfile chart.

1. a. 173,732 sq. mi.   b. 256,750 sq. mi.

2. a. January 27°F, July 64°F   b. January 68°F, July 68°F

3. a. 22 in.   b. 17 in.

4. a. 8,730,289   b. 31,645,896

5. a. 200,500 troops   b. 64,800 troops

6. a. All children between 7 and 16
   b. All children between 7 and 17

3. Work in pairs. Can you remember what else Karl mentions?

🔊 Listen again and check.

GRAMMAR AND FUNCTIONS

Making comparisons (1): comparative and superlative forms of short adjectives

You form the comparative of most short adjectives with -er, and the superlative with -est.

adjective: **old   large   big   dirty**
comparative: *older   larger   bigger   dirtier*
superlative: *oldest   largest   biggest   dirtiest*

There are some irregular comparative and superlative forms.

good   better   best
bad   worse   worst

You use a comparative adjective + than when you compare two things which are different.

*Brazil is **bigger than** Sweden.*

1. How do you form the comparative and superlative of adjectives ending in -e, -y, vowel + -g, and vowel + -t?

2. Write the comparative and superlative forms of these adjectives.

large   fine   close   wide   dirty   dry   healthy   heavy
noisy   big   hot   wet

3. Correct any statements in *Reading and Listening* activity 1 which are false.

The United States is bigger than Brazil.

4. Complete these sentences with the adjective in parentheses.

1. Sweden is _____ than Brazil. (small)
2. Brazil is _____ than Sweden. (hot)
3. The United States is _____ than Brazil. (dry)
4. The United States has the _____ armed services of the three countries. (big)
5. The children in the United States are _____ when they start school than the children in Sweden. (young)
6. Sweden is the _____of the three countries. (cold)

WRITING

Write a factfile for your country. Use the chart in *Reading and Listening* activity 1.
OR
Write a paragraph comparing your country with Brazil, the United States, or Sweden. It doesn't matter if you don't know exact figures.

I think my country is larger than Sweden, but the population is smaller.

10 | Olympic Spirit

**Making comparisons (2): comparative
and superlative forms of longer adjectives**

VOCABULARY AND LISTENING

1. Work in pairs. Which of these sports can you see in the pictures?

> football   auto racing   swimming
> baseball   golf   horseback riding
> climbing   windsurfing   basketball
> skiing   hang gliding   cycling   soccer

Turn to Communication Activity 14 on page 53 and check that you know what the other sports are.

2. Put the words for sports in two columns: *team sports* and *individual sports.*

team sports: football

individual sports: swimming

Now work in pairs and check your answers.

3. Match the adjectives in the box with the sports in the vocabulary box in 1.

> popular   expensive   tiring   dangerous
> fashionable   difficult   exciting

football: popular

Now work in pairs and find out if your partner agrees with you.

4. Look at the statements about sports in the chart. Check (✓) the statements you agree with.

5. 🔲 Listen to Katy and Andy talking about their opinions about sports. Check (✓) the statements they agree with.

6. Work in pairs and check your answers to 5.
🔲 Listen again and check.

GRAMMAR AND FUNCTIONS

> **Making comparisons (2): comparative and superlative forms of longer adjectives**
>
> **You form the comparative of many long adjectives with
> *more* + adjective, and the superlative with *the most* + adjective.**
>
> | adjective: | *expensive* | *tiring* |
> |---|---|---|
> | comparative: | *more expensive* | *more tiring* |
> | superlative: | *the most expensive* | *the most tiring* |
>
> *Climbing is **more difficult** than skiing.*
> *Auto racing is **the most exciting** sport in the world.*

	You	Katy	Andy
The most popular sport is baseball.			
Horseback riding is more expensive than cycling.			
Swimming is the most tiring sport.			
Hang gliding is more dangerous than windsurfing.			
Climbing is more difficult than skiing.			
Auto racing is the most exciting sport.			

1. Complete the sentences using the comparative or superlative form of the adjective.

1. Horseback riding is very expensive.Yes, it's _____ sport I can think of.
2. Auto racing is very dangerous. Yes, it's _____ than skiing.
3. Football is very popular. Yes, it's _____ than golf.
4. Windsurfing is very difficult. Yes, it's one of _____ sports I can think of.
5. Swimming is very tiring. Yes, it's _____ sport in the world.

2. Choose the correct sentence. Can you explain why?

1. a. Soccer is one of the most popular games in the world.
   b. Soccer is one of the popularest games in the world.
2. a. Skiing is the most difficult sport to do well.
   b. Skiing is the more difficult sport to do well.
3. a. The United States is better at soccer than many countries.
   b. The United States is best at soccer than many countries.

3. Work in pairs. Find out how your partner completed the chart in *Vocabulary and Listening* activity 4.

I think hang gliding is the most dangerous sport.
Do you? I think auto racing is more dangerous than hang gliding.

4. Write sentences using the comparative or superlative form of these adjectives.

interesting   lively   boring
intelligent   successful   enjoyable

The most interesting game in the world is chess.

SPEAKING

1. With the rest of the class, make a list of olympic sports.

swimming, gymnastics ...

2. Work in groups of two or three. Find out if people in your class enjoy the Olympic Games. If they enjoy them, what do they like and why? If they don't enjoy them, what do they dislike and why?

Do you like the Olympic Games?
What is the most enjoyable game?
What is the most boring game?

Progress Check 6–10

VOCABULARY

1. When you write down an adjective, make a note of its opposite.

hot – cold   *light – dark*

Match the adjectives and their opposites.
(There may be more than one possibility.)

heavy   large   light   long   round   short   small   square

You may like to look through Lessons 1 to 10 and see if there are other adjectives and their opposites.

2. Work in groups of three or four and play *Word Zigzag* with words from Lessons 6 to 10.

How to play Word Zigzag

1 On a large sheet of paper, Student A writes a word from Lessons 6 to 10 horizontally.

2 Student B thinks of a word which includes one letter from Student A's word and writes it vertically.

3 Student C thinks of another word which includes a letter from Student B's word and writes it horizontally.

4 The game continues until no one can think of a suitable word. The last student to write a word is the winner.

```
                    s t r a i g h t
m o u s t a c h e   h
                    o
                    r
                    t
```

GRAMMAR

1. Choose the correct word in these sentences.

1. Is this *my/mine* pen? No, it's *my/mine*.
2. Whose are these? They're *her/hers*.
3. Where did you leave *your/yours* coat?
4. This isn't *their/theirs*. It's *your/yours*.
5. Have you got *my/mine* ticket?
6. These are *my/mine* gloves, not *your/yours*.

2. Write the comparative and superlative forms of the following adjectives.

large   good   popular   big   comfortable   healthy
safe   wet   expensive   tiring   heavy   high   difficult

large   larger   largest

3. Complete these sentences with the comparative form of the adjective in parentheses.

1. Mexico is _____ than the United States. (small)
2. Parachuting is _____ than skiing. (dangerous)
3. Hang gliding is _____ than windsurfing. (expensive)
4. Winter in Canada is _____ than winter in Brazil. (cold)
5. Soccer is _____ than boxing. (popular)
6. Cycling is _____ than hang gliding. (exciting)

4. Complete the sentences using the comparative or superlative form of the adjective.

1. Alaska is a very large state. Yes, it's the _____ state in the United States.
2. Auto racing is very expensive. Yes, it's the _____ sport I can think of.
3. Switzerland is a small country. Yes, it's _____ than Sweden.
4. Swimming is a tiring sport. Yes, it's _____ than baseball.
5. Soccer is a very popular sport. Yes, it's the _____ sport in the world.

5. Write two words to complete the following sentences.

1. I feel _____.
2. My _____ hurt/hurts.
3. I have _____.

6. Reply to these people and give advice. Use *should/shouldn't.*

1. I'm tired.
2. I have a toothache.
3. My back hurts.
4. I feel sick.
5. I have a cold.
6. I have a cough.

SOUNDS

1. Group the words which rhyme.

could   half   said   head   wood   red   laugh   good

📼 Listen and check. As you listen, say the words out loud.

2. Say these words out loud. Is the underlined sound /eɪ/ or /aɪ/?

f<u>a</u>ce   f<u>i</u>ne   s<u>i</u>gn   M<u>ay</u>   <u>ei</u>ght   n<u>igh</u>t   l<u>ie</u>   m<u>ai</u>d   tr<u>ay</u>

📼 Listen and check. As you listen, say the words out loud.

3. Match the words and the stress patterns.

☐ ▢ ▢   ▢ ☐ ▢   ▢ ☐ ▢ ▢

reception   windsurfing   rectangular   receiver
umbrella   temperature

📼 Listen and check. As you listen, say the words out loud.

4. Underline the words you think the speakers will stress.

CUSTOMER	And I must have lost it then.
OFFICIAL	Just say your name again, ma'am.
CUSTOMER	Mary Walter.
OFFICIAL	May I have your address and phone number?
CUSTOMER	E 23010 'E' Street, Toronto. 758-8956.
OFFICIAL	And it was a black plastic bag, right?
CUSTOMER	Yes.
OFFICIAL	And you last saw it on March 20 at two in the afternoon?
CUSTOMER	Yes, in the grocery store.
OFFICIAL	And what was in it?
CUSTOMER	All my shopping and my purse.

📼 Listen and check.

SPEAKING

1. Work in groups of three or four. Look at these sentences and decide what the situation is.

1. I have a sore throat.
2. Do you have it in red?
3. When did you lose it?
4. My back hurts.
5. Yes, I'm trying to make a phone call, but there's no dial tone.

2. Match the sentences in 1 with the replies below.

a. This morning.
b. Not in your size, I'm afraid.
c. Yes, it does look a little bit red.
d. Well, you really shouldn't carry that.
e. What number were you calling?

3. Choose one or two conversations and write a few sentences to continue them. When you're ready, act them out to the rest of the class.

11 | *When in Rome, Do As the Romans Do*

Talking about obligation: *have to/don't have to/should(n't)/can('t)*

VOCABULARY AND READING

1. Work in pairs. Use the words in the box to say what's happening in the pictures.

> shake hands   cover   point at
> kiss   take off

2. Read *When in Rome* and match the rules and advice with the pictures.

When in Rome

- [ ] In parts of Africa you have to ask if you want to take a photograph of someone.
- [ ] In Japan you have to take off your shoes when you go into someone's home.
- [ ] In Saudi Arabia women have to cover their heads in public.
- [ ] In the U.S. you shouldn't point at people.
- [ ] In Japan you shouldn't look people in the eye.
- [ ] In China you shouldn't kiss in public.
- [ ] In Taiwan you should give a gift with both hands.
- [ ] In South America you should shake hands when you meet someone.

LISTENING

1. 🔲 Listen to James, who's Australian, talking about some of the advice and rules in *When in Rome*. Check (✓) the statements he talks about.

2. Look at these sentences.

Women don't have to cover their heads in Australia.

In Australia you can look people in the eye.

Complete these sentences with *don't have to* and *can* so that they are true for Australia.

1. You _____ ask if you want to take a photograph of someone.
2. You _____ take your shoes off when you go into someone's house in Australia.
3. You _____ kiss in public in Australia.
4. You _____ shake hands with everyone when you meet them in Australia. You _____ shake hands when you meet someone for the first time.

3. 🔲 Now listen again and check.

GRAMMAR

Talking about obligation

You use *have to* if it is necessary to do something.
*You **have to** take off your shoes when you go into someone's house.*

You use *don't have to* if it's not necessary to do something.
*In Australia, women **don't have to** cover their heads in public.*

You use *should* if it's a good idea to do something.
*You **should** give a gift with both hands.*

You use *shouldn't* if it's not a good idea to do something.
*In China you **shouldn't** kiss in public.*

You use *can* if it's OK to do something.
*You **can** kiss in public, but not many people do.*

You use *can't* if you're not allowed to do something.
*You **can't** park your car here.*

Can and ***should*** are modal verbs. For more information about modal verbs see Grammar Review page 58.**

1. Complete these sentences with *have to* or *don't have to*.

1. Children _____ be quiet all the time.
2. You _____ be quiet in a library.
3. You _____ go through customs when you enter the United States.
4. Men _____ take off their coats in a church.
5. You _____ take your shoes off in an Australian home.
6. You _____ wear a uniform to university in the United States.

2. Write some advice for people learning a foreign language.

You have to come to classes every week.
You shouldn't miss any class.

3. Write some rules for your school or the place where you work.

You can't smoke during class.

SPEAKING AND WRITING

1. Work in pairs. Think of advice you can give to visitors to your country about the following:

– giving presents   – what to wear
– table manners   – eating habits
– visiting someone's home

When you receive a gift in Mexico, you should open it immediately.

2. Work with another pair. Do you have similar rules and advice? Write a list of advice and rules for visitors to your country.

12 *Have You Ever Been to San Francisco?*

Present perfect (1): talking about experiences

READING AND VOCABULARY

1. Look at these famous sights of San Francisco. Do you know what they are?

2. Read this postcard from San Francisco. Which picture is on the back of it?

Dear David and Anna,

Hi! How are you? We're having a wonderful time in San Francisco. We're staying in a hotel in the center of the city. We've only been here four days but we've done so much already. We've watched a Giants game at Candlestick Park and we've taken a cable car downtown (you can see one on this postcard). We've visited Chinatown, but not Alcatraz. We've climbed Telegraph Hill and we've been to Fisherman's Wharf, but we haven't been to the Golden Gate Bridge yet. We're going there tomorrow.

See you soon!

Love Doug and Debbie

David and Anna Sayle
Apartment 214
51st West City
Street
New York 10021
U.S.A.

3. Here is a list of some of the things you can do in San Francisco. Check (✓) the places Doug and Debbie have been to or the things they've done.

- [ ] watch a Giants game
- [ ] visit Alcatraz
- [ ] visit Chinatown
- [ ] take a cable car
- [ ] climb Telegraph Hill
- [ ] go to the Golden Gate Bridge

4. Complete the sentences below with the words in the box.

| climb | hill | bridge | park | view |

1. A _____ is a small mountain.
2. You cross a river by going over a _____.
3. When you _____ something, you go up it.
4. A _____ is a public place, with trees and grass.
5. The _____ from a building is what you can see from it.

SOUNDS

1. 🔲 Listen and repeat.

ever   Have you ever   Have you ever been
Have you ever been to San Francisco?
ever   Have you ever   Have you ever stayed
Have you ever stayed in a hotel?

2. 🔲 Read and listen to this conversation.
Underline the stressed words.

A Have you ever been to San Francisco?
B No, I haven't. I've never been there.
A Have you ever stayed in a hotel?
B Yes, I have.
A When was that?
B When I was in Mexico last year.

3. Work in pairs and practice the conversation in 2.

GRAMMAR

Present perfect (1): talking about experiences
You use the present perfect to talk about an experience, often with *ever* and *never*.
***Have you ever stayed** in a hotel?*
(= Do you have the experience of staying in a hotel?)
Yes, I have. (= Yes, at some time in my life, but it's not important when.)
*No, I haven't. **I've never stayed** in a hotel.*
You form the present perfect with *has/have* + past participle. You usually use the contracted form, *'ve* or *'s*. Many past participles are irregular.
*Have you ever **been** to San Francisco? We've **done** so much.*
Remember that you use the past simple to talk about a definite time in the past.
When did you stay in a hotel? When I was in Mexico last year.

1. Work in pairs. Ask and answer questions about what Doug and Debbie have done on their vacation.

1. watch a Giants game
2. visit Chinatown
3. climb Telegraph Hill
4. visit Alcatraz
5. take a cable car
6. go to the Golden Gate Bridge

1. Have they watched a Giants game?
Yes, they have.

2. Here are the regular past participles of some verbs. Write the infinitive.

lived   worked   stayed   watched   visited   listened

3. Match the infinitives with their irregular past participles.

eat   drink   drive   read   see   fly   take   buy   win
make   write   send

driven   sent   read   seen   flown   bought   won
made   eaten   drunk   taken   written

WRITING

Imagine you're a visitor to your town. Write a postcard to a friend saying what you've seen and where you've been. Use the postcard in *Reading and Vocabulary* activity 2 to help you.

Dear Henrique,

Hi, how are you? I'm in Rio de Janeiro right now. I've been to Copacabana beach…

Present perfect (2): talking about unfinished events; *for* and *since*

VOCABULARY AND LISTENING

1. You are going to read and listen to Ben and Abby, who live in New York, talking about their city. Which of these words do you expect to see?

> anniversary cash celebrate crime deli disco
> golden immigrant neighborhood retire rob
> sight subway war

2. Look at the conversation with Ben and Abby. Decide where the sentences a–e go in the conversation.

   a. It was love at first sight!

   b. I've been here for fifty-one years.

   c. You want to see China?

   d. Have you ever been robbed?

   e. I haven't been out of New York since the war

Abby and Ben Goldman live in Brooklyn, New York. They have a small deli and grocery store by the river. The deli is famous because it is open every day of the year, including Christmas Day, and because the sandwiches are so good!

INTERVIEWER	Have you always worked here?
ABBY	Yes, my father opened the deli the year I was born, in 1922, and I started work when I was fourteen.
INTERVIEWER	What about you, Ben?
BEN	Well, I started here just after the war, in 1946, so (1) _____
INTERVIEWER	And when did you get married?
ABBY	In 1947. (2) _____ We just celebrated our golden wedding anniversary.
BEN	Yes, we've been married for fifty years. Such a long time…
INTERVIEWER	Well, congratulations! Tell me about life in New York.
ABBY	I've lived in New York all my life. It's the greatest city in the world!
INTERVIEWER	What do you like about it?
ABBY	Oh, it's so interesting. There are so many different people, there's Coney Island, and Central Park, and our neighbors are great. Really great. We've lived right here

	in this neighborhood since we got married.
BEN	And there's every kind of food, from all over the world.
INTERVIEWER	But what about the crime? (3) _____
ABBY	Oh yes! But we don't keep much cash here, so…
BEN	There are bad people everywhere you go.
INTERVIEWER	Have you ever wanted to live somewhere else? To travel around the world?
BEN	Why? You can see the world right here! (4) _____ Go to Chinatown! You want to see Italy? Go to Little Italy! It's all here. (5) _____ and I'm very happy.
ABBY	I've always wanted to go to France, though… to Paris. Maybe after we retire…
INTERVIEWER	And when will that be?
BEN	Retire? Me? Never!
ABBY	He always says that.

3. 🔲 Listen and check your answers to 2.

4. Work in groups of three and act out the conversation.

GRAMMAR

> Present perfect (2): talking about unfinished events; *for* and *since*
>
> **You use the present perfect to talk about an unfinished event, something that started in the past and continues now.**
>
> *We've been married for fifty years.* (= We got married fifty years ago, and we are still married.)
>
> *I've lived in New York all my life.* (= I still live in New York.)
>
> **You use *for* to talk about how long something has continued.**
>
> *I've been here for fifty-one years.*
>
> **You use *since* to talk about when something started.**
>
> *We've lived here in this neighborhood since we got married.*

1. Answer these questions about the conversation in *Vocabulary and Listening* activity 2. Use *since*.

1. How long has Abby worked at the deli?
2. How long has Ben worked at the deli?
3. How long have Abby and Ben been married?
4. How long have they lived in Brooklyn?
5. How long has the deli been open?

1. She has worked at the deli since 1936.

2. Answer the questions in 1. Use *for*.

1. She has worked at the deli for 61 years.

3. Choose the correct sentence. Can you explain why?

1. a. They *been* married for twelve years.
   b. They *'ve been* married for twelve years.
2. a. When I *was* a child, I lived in Florida.
   b. When I *'ve been* a child, I lived in Florida.
3. a. She's been here *since* eight o'clock this morning.
   b. She's been here *for* eight o'clock this morning.
4. a. He *went* shopping yesterday.
   b. He*'s been* shopping yesterday.
5. a. *Have you worked* here for a long time?
   b. *Do you work* here for a long time?
6. a. I *study* English for two years.
   b. I*'ve studied* English for two years.

SPEAKING AND WRITING

1. Find out about your partner. Ask questions and complete the chart about your partner.

What do you do? How long have you been a...

	Your partner
Name	
Married	
Jobs	
Children	
Town	
Moved there	

2. Now write a short paragraph about your partner using the information in the chart.

Planning the Perfect Day

Imperatives; infinitive of purpose

SPEAKING

1. Work in pairs. What is your idea of a perfect day out? Here are some suggestions:

– a shopping trip
– a day at the beach
– a picnic in the countryside
– a tour of an historic building
– a day with some friends
– a walk in the mountains

2. Look at the picture. Which of the situations in 1 does it show?

4. Work in pairs. Do you agree with the advice in the passage? Do you have picnics like this in your country?

READING AND VOCABULARY

1. Work in pairs. Make a list of things to do or take on a perfect picnic.

2. Read *The Perfect Picnic* and decide which paragraph mentions the things in the picture.

3. Match these words with the pictures.

bottle opener barbecue matches knife fork cup carton trash blanket cooler

The Perfect Picnic

Everyone says that food and drink taste better when you have a picnic. But what do you do to have a perfect picnic? Here's some advice.

I. Choose where you want to go very carefully. In the countryside? In the city? The picnic site should be attractive and interesting, to be sure there's something to do when you finish your picnic.

2. Check the weather forecast the day before you go. The perfect picnic needs perfect weather.

3. Don't take too much to carry. For the perfect picnic you leave home with food and drink and you return only with trash.

4. Choose small items of food, such as eggs or sandwiches, to avoid taking knives and forks. To make it the perfect picnic, take food which you don't usually eat.

5. Take small cartons of juice or refillable plastic bottles of water. They're more expensive, but they aren't as heavy as glass bottles, cups, and glasses.

6. Pack a blanket to sit on or, if it's cold, to keep you warm.

7. Put fresh food and cold drinks in a small cooler to keep them cool.

8. Put the whole picnic in a lot of of small bags, to allow everyone to carry something.

9. Prepare everything before you go OR make sure you've got everything you need to finish preparing the picnic, such as a knife, a bottle opener, barbecue, and matches.

10. Check that there is a short walk to the picnic site to make people hungry.

GRAMMAR

> **Imperatives**
>
> **You use an imperative (infinitive without *to*) to give instructions and advice.**
> *Check the weather forecast.*
>
> **You use *don't* + imperative for a negative instruction.**
> *Don't take too much to carry.*
>
> **Infinitive of purpose**
>
> **You use *to* + infinitive:**
>
> – **to say why people do things.**
> *Try to have your picnic on a weekday, **to avoid** the weekend traffic.*
>
> – **to say what you use something to do.**
> *You use a bottle opener **to open** bottles.*

1. Answer the questions. Use *to* + infinitive.

1. Why should the picnic site be attractive and interesting?
2. Why should you choose small items of food?
3. Why should you pack a blanket?
4. Why should you put fresh food in a cooler?
5. Why should you put the whole picnic in a lot of small bags?
6. Why should you check that there's a short walk to the picnic site?

1. To be sure there's something to do when you finish your picnic.

2. Match words in the vocabulary box in *Reading and Vocabulary* activity 3 with what you use them to do.

1. to put food in your mouth   4. to keep something cold
2. to cook food outdoors   5. to light a barbecue
3. to cut food   6. to sit on or to keep you warm

3. Work in pairs and check your answers to 2.

You use a fork to put food in your mouth.

4. Think of reasons why you do the following. Use *to* + infinitive.

1. go shopping   4. go to work/school
2. take a vacation   5. go to a movie
3. go to the airport   6. use a knife

1. You go shopping to buy food or clothes.

WRITING

1. Work in groups of two or three. You're going to prepare some advice for planning the perfect day out. Make sure you all choose the same situation from *Speaking* activity 1.

First, work alone. Make notes on your advice.

a shopping trip – make a list

2. Work with the rest of the group. Make a list of all your advice, and explain why. Use an imperative and *to* + infinitive.

Write a list of things to buy to make sure that you don't forget anything.

3. Show your instructions to another group. Do they agree with your advice? Is there anything which surprises them?

15 She Sings Well

Adverbs

Antonia	
Music	She sings well and she plays the piano and guitar beautifully.
Art	She draws very carefully. Her work is excellent.
General	She is a very artistic young woman.

Carlos	
Sport	He can run quickly, and plays tennis well. He's good at most sports.
English	He writes very slowly and his spelling is very bad
General	He finds many subjects very difficult. Must try harder.

Trudy	
Maths	She can add and subtract numbers quickly in her head.
Science	She is good at biology. She passed the exam easily.
General	Beate shows great ability in her work.

Kate	
French	She speaks French almost fluently. Well done!
English	She writes English compositions confidently. She works very hard.
General	Her manners are excellent. She talks to people quietly and politely.

VOCABULARY

1. Match the adverbs and their opposites in the box below.

> badly carefully carelessly quickly
> loudly politely quietly rudely
> slowly well

2. 🔲 Listen to four conversations. Which adverbs would you use to describe how the speakers are speaking?

READING AND SPEAKING

1. Work in pairs. Look at the pictures. What do you think the people do?

2. Work in pairs. Who do you think was good at school?

3. Work in pairs. Read the extracts from these high school report cards and match the adults in the pictures with the children in the report cards.

4. Say what the people were good at when they were in high school.

Antonia was good at music.

5. Work in pairs and say what you were good at when you were in school.

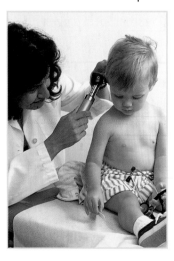

GRAMMAR

> Adverbs
>
> **You use an adverb to describe a verb.**
> *She speaks **slowly**.*
> **You usually form an adverb by adding -ly to the adjective.**
> *quiet – quietly*
> *loud – loudly*
> **If the adjective ends in -y, you drop the -y and add -ily.**
> *easy – easily*
> **Some adverbs have the same form as the adjective they come from.**
> *late   early   hard   fast*
> **The adverb from the adjective *good* is *well*.**
> *She's a **good** singer. She sings **well**.*

1. Write the adjectives which the adverbs in the vocabulary box come from.

badly – bad

2. Write the adverbs which come from these adjectives.

angry happy gentle immediate successful comfortable sudden dangerous frequent

3. Complete the sentences with the adjective in parentheses or the adverb which comes from it.

1. He spoke _____ so everyone could hear him _____.
   (clear, good)
2. They were late so they had a _____ game of handball and then left. (quick)
3. She had a very _____ class with her students. (successful)
4. He listened to his teacher very _____. (careful)
5. Could you speak more _____, please? Your accent is _____ to understand. (slow, hard)
6. He passed the oral exam very _____. (easy)

4. Work in pairs. Say what people in your class can do and how well they do it. Use an adverb.

Geraldo can run quickly.

LISTENING AND SPEAKING

1. Think about your answers to these questions about school.

	You	**Joel**	**Patrice**
Do/did you always work very hard?			
Do/did you always listen carefully to your teachers?			
Do/did you always behave very well?			
Do/did you pass your tests easily?			
Do/did you always write slowly and carefully?			
Do you think schooldays are/were the best days of your life?			

2. 🔲 Listen to Joel and Patrice answering the questions. Put a check (✓) by the ones they say *yes* to.

3. Work in pairs and check your answers to 2. Can you remember what Joel and Patrice said in detail?
🔲 Now listen again and check.

4. Work in pairs. Ask your partner the questions in the chart.

Progress Check 11–15

VOCABULARY

1. A collocation is two or more words which often go together.

fast car   high mountain   busy street   have dinner

Here are some adjectives from Lessons 11 to 15.

cold   difficult   low   old   expensive

Think of nouns which often go with the adjectives. You can use your dictionary.

cold day

2. There may be many places outside your classroom where you can see and listen to English, and build your vocabulary. In which of the following places can you see or hear English words?

– on food labels
– at the airport
– on billboards and signs
– in instruction manuals (e.g. for electrical things)
– at the bus or train station
– on the radio
– on travel documents (tickets, etc.)
– on TV
– in newspapers

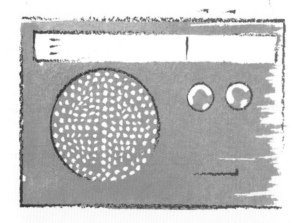

GRAMMAR

1. Complete these sentences from Lesson 11 with *should(n't)* or *have to.*

1. In parts of Africa you _____ ask if you want to take a photograph of someone.
2. In Saudi Arabia women _____ cover their heads in public.
3. In China you _____ kiss in public.
4. In Japan you _____ look people in the eye.
5. In Taiwan you _____ give a gift with both hands.
6. In the United States you _____ point at people.

2. Write sentences saying why you:

1. use a blanket   4. use a match
2. go to the swimming pool   5. use a bottle opener
3. go to the grocery store   6. use the phone

1. You use a blanket to keep warm.

3. Write the adverbs which come from these adjectives.

easy   good   careful   fast   hard   polite   quiet   rude

4. Complete the sentences with the adjective in parentheses or the adverb which comes from it.

1. She speaks English very _____. (good)
2. He drives really _____. (fast)
3. He's really _____ to people. (polite)
4. Don't make so much noise. Please be _____. (quiet)
5. Japanese is a _____ language to learn. (hard)
6. He passed his TOEFL exam _____.(easy)

SOUNDS

1. Group the words with the same vowel sound.

beer   stair   hair   near   hear   chair   air   we're   year

🔊 Listen and check. As you listen, say the words out loud.

2. Say these words out loud. Is the underlined sound /əʊ/ or /ɔː/?

s<u>o</u>   J<u>o</u>   t<u>o</u>re   w<u>a</u>r   g<u>o</u>   fl<u>oo</u>r   l<u>o</u>w   s<u>o</u>re   t<u>o</u>e   sp<u>o</u>rt

🔊 Listen and check. As you listen, say the words out loud.

3. 🔊 Listen to how you can change the stressed word in a question and get a different answer.

1. a. Can you **speak** Spanish?
      No, but I can **write** it.
   b. Can you speak **Spanish**?
      No, but I can speak **Italian**.

2. a. Did you stay with friends in **Rio**?
      No, I stayed with friends in **Belo Horizonte**.
   b. Did you stay with **friends** in Rio?
      No, I stayed in a **hotel**.

3. a. Do you have **this dress** in another color?
      No, only **that** one.
   b. Do you have this dress in another **color**?
      No, we only have it in **red**.

READING

1. Look at the pictures below. Can you guess what happens in the story? Now read the story and see if you guessed correctly.

2. Read the story again and cross out any words which aren't "necessary." You cannot cross out two or more words together.

> A young man went into a local bank, went up to the woman teller and gave her a note and a plastic bag. The note said, "Put all your money into this bag, please." The middle-aged teller was very frightened so she gave him all the money. He put it in his bag and ran out of the front door. When he got back home the city police were there. His note was on an old, white envelope and on the envelope was his home address.

3. Work in pairs and check your answers to 2.

4. Work in pairs and choose a short passage from *Move Up* Elementary.

Working alone, count the number of "unnecessary" words in the passage.

Tell each other how many words you've found. Who has found the most?

16 | *Cruisin'!*

Future simple (1): *(will)* for decisions

VOCABULARY AND SOUNDS

1. Look at the words in the box. Put them under two headings: *ship* and *plane*. Use a dictionary, if necessary.

> departure lounge   passport control   baggage reclaim
> port   check-in   arrival hall   boarding pass   on board
> cruise   business class   first class   round-trip   one-way
> departure gate   travel agency   economy class

2. Listen to these two-word nouns. Underline the stressed word.

departure lounge   passport control   business class
travel agency   arrival hall

Now say the words out loud.

LISTENING

1. Look at this conversation. Where does it take place?

A May I help you?
B Yes, I need a flight to New York.
A One-way or round-trip?
B Round-trip.
A When do you want to travel? It's cheaper if you spend Saturday night in New York.
B I'll go on Thursday and come back on Monday, then.
A And will that be economy or business class?
B Oh, I'll take business class, please.
A OK, that's going to be $259.66. How would you like to pay?
B Do you take checks?
A No, ma'am, only credit cards.
B OK, I'll use my Visa card, then. Oh, can you arrange a rental car for me at the airport?
A Yes, of course. We can get you a small car for $24.50 a day.
B Perfect! For four days then.
A So, that'll be $357.66 total.
B Thanks.

2. Listen and underline anything which is different from what you hear.

GRAMMAR

> **Future simple (1):** *(will)* for decisions
>
> **You form the future simple with** *will* **or** *won't* **+ infinitive.**
>
> | I you he/she/it we they | 'll (will) won't (will not) | go on Thursday. |
> |---|---|---|
>
> **You use** *will* **when you make a decision at the time of speaking.**
>
> *I'll take business class.*   *I'll use my credit card.*

1. Work in pairs.

Student A: You're going to act out the conversation in *Listening* activity 1. You're in the travel agency. Change some of the details in the conversation.

Student B: You're going to act out the conversation in *Listening* activity 1. You're the passenger. Change some of the details about the ticket you want to buy.

2. Act out the conversation when you're ready.

READING AND SPEAKING

1. Read the travel brochure and follow the route on the map.

2. Imagine you want to go on the cruise described in the travel brochure. Look at the brochure and answer the questions.

  1. How long will you spend on *The Seaworthy*?

  2. How long will you spend in Trinidad and Tobago?

  3. Will you have to pay for meals on *The Seaworthy*?

  4. How will you get from Jamaica to Miami?

  5. Will you be able to have a room by yourself on *The Seaworthy*?

  6. Will you be able to practice golf on the cruise?

  7. Will you have to pay anything extra?

  8. Will you be able to play tennis?

3. Work in groups of three.

Student A: Turn to Communication Activity 10 on page 52.

Student B: Turn to Communication Activity 5 on page 51.

Student C: Turn to Communication Activity 12 on page 53.

LUXURY TRAVEL, INC. PRESENTS
14-DAY CARIBBEAN CRUISE

Visiting the beautiful tropical islands of Antigua, Barbados, Trinidad, Tobago, Curaçao, Aruba, and Jamaica on board the luxury ship *The Seaworthy*

FOR ONLY $1542 per person

ITINERARY

Day 1 Take the plane from Miami to San Juan, Puerto Rico.

Day 2–3 Join *The Seaworthy* and sail overnight to the island of Antigua.

Day 4 Spend the day in Antigua. Sail overnight to Barbados.

Day 5 Explore Barbados. Scuba diving lesson. Sail at night for Trinidad.

Day 6–7 Visit the islands of Trinidad and Tobago.

Day 8 Cruise the South Caribbean Sea.

Day 9 Sightseeing on the island of Curaçao.

Day 10 Explore the island of Aruba.

Day 11 Sail for Jamaica.

Day 12–13 Relax on the island of Jamaica at the *Tropicana Hotel* in Port Antonio.

Day 14 Take the plane back to Miami.

Accommodation in double suites (single suites available at an additional charge). Extra nights' accommodation in Jamaica available.

Facilities on board: two swimming pools, a volleyball and basketball court, and a golf driving net, an elegant dining room with five-star cuisine, and marvellous places to dance. All suites have remote-controlled satellite television and video cassette players.

Price per person includes air travel, all meals on *The Seaworthy*, bed and breakfast at *The Tropicana* and all transport to and from airports. Travel insurance, and on-island transport not included.

17 | *What Will It Be Like in the Future?*

Future simple (2): *(will)* for predictions

VOCABULARY AND LISTENING

1. Match the words in the box with the weather symbols.

fog cloud sun rain wind snow

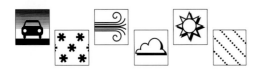

2. Which of these adjectives can you use to describe today's weather?

cold cool dry foggy hot rainy sunny
warm wet windy snowy

It's very hot today.

3. Look at the pictures and say what the weather is like.

4. 📼 Work in pairs. Look at the newspaper weather report below and listen to the radio weather forecast. Underline any information which is different from what you hear.

Worldwide forecast for noon tomorrow

Athens	c	54
Bangkok	c	86
Cairo	s	61
Geneva	c	40
Hong Kong	c	62
Istanbul	r	44
Kuala Lumpur	c	86
Lisbon	c	52
Madrid	r	44
Moscow	sn	14
New York	s	32
Paris	sn	43
Prague	sn	28
Rio	c	84
Rome	r	48
Tokyo	c	40
Warsaw	c	17

GRAMMAR

> **Future simple (2):** *(will)* for predictions
> **You form the future simple with *will* + infinitive. You use the future simple to make predictions.**
> *It'll be* sunny in New York tomorrow.
> (= It will be sunny in New York tomorrow.)
> *It won't be* rainy. (= It will not be rainy.)
> *Will it be snowy in New York?*   Yes, it will.
> *Will it rain in Rio?*   No, it won't.

1. Work in pairs. Correct your answers to *Vocabulary and Listening* activity 4.

In Geneva, it will be cloudy and fifty degrees.

2. Look at the weather report again. Make comparisons between the weather in these cities.

1. Cairo – Tokyo
2. Athens – Rome
3. Warsaw – Moscow
4. Bangkok – Lisbon
5. Prague – Madrid
6. Istanbul – Athens

1. It'll be hotter in Cairo than in Tokyo.

3. Write a short forecast for tomorrow's weather in your town.

Tomorrow it'll be sunny in the morning and cloudy in the evening.

READING AND SPEAKING

1. Look at these predictions about the weather. Do you think they are true for your country?

In twenty-five years:
– it'll be colder
– the sea level will be lower
– it'll be windier
– it'll be wetter
– there'll be more snow

2. Read *Turning Up the Heat* and find out if the predictions are true for the United States.

Turning Up the Heat

A government report says that in the next fifty years, North America will get warmer and have higher sea levels. The Southwest will become drier, and the Midwest will have more rain and floods. Strong winds and hurricanes will become more common. This will be bad for farmers, because crops will not grow as well, so food prices will go up. But the warmer temperatures will make parts of Alaska and Canada greener and better for farming. The higher sea level will mean that many cities, including Seattle, San Francisco, New York, and Miami will disappear under water, and fresh water will be hard to find in some areas. Many people will move to the mountains to live.

Winters will not be so cold, so people will only use heating in their homes for two or three months of the year, but houses will cost more because good land will be hard to find.

3. Here are some more worldwide predictions. Which do you think will be true?

1. Temperatures will rise by four to ten degrees Fahrenheit in fifty years.
2. Ice at the North and South Pole will melt.
3. Whole countries will disappear underwater.
4. There won't be enough fresh water for everyone.
5. Fresh water will cost more.
6. Manufactured goods will cost more to produce.
7. The world economy will get worse.

4. Work in groups of two or three. Make other predictions about the future.

There'll be more people in the world.

18 *Hamlet Was Written by Shakespeare*

Active and passive

SPEAKING AND VOCABULARY

1. Work in pairs. Are these sentences true or false?

Apple makes computers.
Lemons grow on trees.
Gustav Eiffel built the Eiffel Tower.
Marconi invented the radio.
Beethoven composed the Moonlight Sonata.
Leonardo da Vinci painted the Mona Lisa *(La Joconde)*.
Shakespeare wrote Hamlet.
Fleming discovered penicillin.

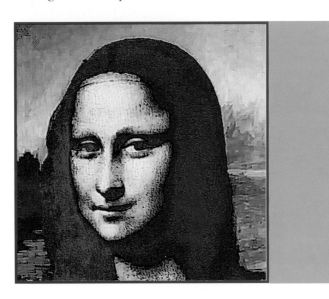

2. Complete these sentences with verbs from the box.
You may have to change the tense.

> make   grow   build   invent   compose   paint
> write   discover

1. Botticelli _____ *La Primavera*.
2. They _____ oranges in Florida.
3. Marie Curie _____ radioactivity.
4. Shah Jehan _____ the Taj Mahal.
5. Homer _____ the Odyssey.
6. They _____ Honda cars in Japan.
7. The Chinese _____ gunpowder.
8. Tchaikovsky _____ the *1812 Symphony*.

READING

1. Read *The Round-the-World Quiz* and choose the correct answer.

The Round-the-World Quiz

1. Coffee is grown in…
a. Brazil   b. Canada   c. Sweden

2. Daewoo cars are made in…
a. Switzerland   b. Thailand   c. Korea

3. Sony computers are made in…
a. Japan   b. the U.S.A.   c. Germany

4. Tea is grown in…
a. India   b. France   c. England

5. Tobacco is grown in…
a. Norway   b. Iceland   c. the U.S.A.

6. Benetton clothes are made in…
a. Italy   b. France   c. Malaysia

7. Roquefort cheese is made in…
a. Germany   b. Thailand   c. France

8. The atom bomb was invented by…
a. the Japanese   b. the Americans   c. the Chinese

9. *Guernica* was painted by…
a. Picasso   b. Turner   c. Monet

10. The Caribbean islands were discovered by…
a. Neil Armstrong   b. Christopher Columbus
c. Marco Polo

11. The telephone was invented by…
a. Bell   b. Marconi   c. Baird

12. *Romeo and Juliet* was written by…
a. Ibsen   b. Shakespeare   c. Stephen King

13. The Blue Mosque in Istanbul was built for…
a. Sultan Ahmet   b. Ataturk
c. Suleyman the Magnificent

14. *Yesterday* was composed by…
a. Paul McCartney   b. John Lennon   c. Mick Jagger

15. The Pyramids were built by…
a. the Pharaohs   b. the Sultans   c. Walt Disney

2. Work in pairs. Check your answers to the quiz.

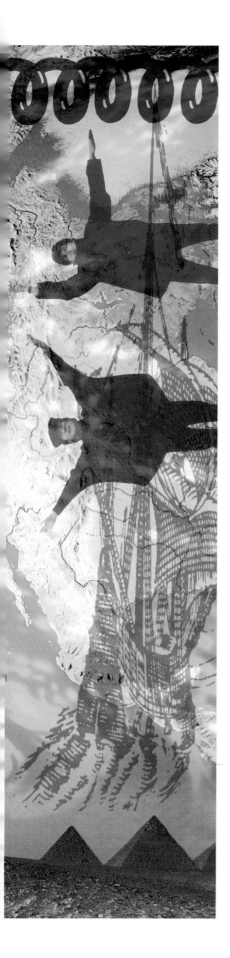

GRAMMAR

Active and passive	
Active	**Passive**
They **grow** *coffee in Brazil.*	*Coffee* **is grown** *in Brazil.*
The Americans **invented** *the atom bomb.*	*The atom bomb* **was invented** *by the Americans.*
You form the passive with the verb *to be* **+ past participle. You use** *by* **to say who or what is responsible for an action.**	
Present simple	**Past simple**
Tea **is grown** *in India.*	*Guernica* **was painted by** *Picasso.*
Daewoo cars **are made** *in Korea.*	*The Pyramids* **were built by** *the Pharaohs.*

1. Look at the quiz again. Find examples of the passive. Are they in the present or past simple?

Sony computers are made in Japan. (present)

2. Choose six sentences from the quiz and rewrite them as active sentences.

Bell invented the telephone. They grow tobacco in the U.S.A.

3. Rewrite the sentences in *Speaking and Vocabulary* activity 2 in the passive.

La Primavera was painted by Botticelli.

LISTENING

1. 🔲 Listen to Frank and Sally doing *The Round-the-World Quiz*. Check (✓) the correct answers. What's their score?

2. How many correct answers did you get?

WRITING AND SPEAKING

1. Work in pairs. Write a quiz about your country.

The Chapel Royal in the Wat Phrae Kaew was built by...
a. King Rama 1   b. King Rama IV   c. King Rama V

Make sure you include one correct answer and two incorrect ones.

2. Work with another pair. Do each other's quizzes.

19 | *She Said It Wasn't Far*

Reported speech: statements

LISTENING AND READING

1. Decide where these sentences go in the conversation.

   a. it leaves at nine o'clock.

   b. And where's the nearest campsite?

   c. Where are you walking to?

   d. No, not really, it's two miles.

   e. We'll stay for just one night.

CHRIS Good afternoon.

RECEPTIONIST Hi there! Can I help you?

CHRIS Do you have any beds for tonight?

RECEPTIONIST Yes, I think so. You see, I just started work at the hostel. How long would you like to stay?

CHRIS (1) _____

RECEPTIONIST Yes, that's OK.

TONY Great!

RECEPTIONIST How old are you?

TONY We're both sixteen.

RECEPTIONIST OK, that'll be $13 each.

CHRIS Is it far from the hostel to Eureka?

RECEPTIONIST (2) _____ It takes about an hour on foot.

TONY Is there a bus?

RECEPTIONIST I think so. It takes about fifteen minutes. There's a bus every hour.

TONY What time is the last bus from Eureka?

RECEPTIONIST I think (3) _____ There's not much to do at night.

CHRIS We're exhausted! We need to go to bed early. What time does the hostel close in the morning?

RECEPTIONIST Umm, at eleven A.M. (4) _____

CHRIS We're going to Crescent City. Are you serving dinner tonight?

RECEPTIONIST Yes, we're serving dinner until eight o'clock. And breakfast starts at seven thirty.

TONY (5) _____

RECEPTIONIST I'm not sure. I think it's Fortuna, which is about ten miles north of here. I started work last Monday so I'm very new here.

2. 🔲 Listen and check.

3. The receptionist gives Chris and Tony some wrong information. Read the brochure and underline the wrong information in the conversation.

**Redwoods Youth Hostel,
Goldmine Avenue, Eureka, CA 90612**
Tel (707) 516-4848 Fax (707) 516-4800

Facilities
40 beds
Open 24 hours, all year
Outdoor hot tub
No family rooms
Recreation room
Washing machines
No smoking hostel
Campsites available

Charges
Under 18 $12 Adult $16

Meal times
Breakfast 7 A.M
Dinner 6 P.M. – 7 P.M.

Travel Information
Town center three miles
Bus service to Eureka No.14
(takes ten minutes) Last bus 8 P.M.

Nearest campsites
Fortuna 8 miles (south)
Aracata 15 miles (north)

---

4. 🔘 Listen and number the next part of the conversation in the order you hear it.

TONY Yes, and she said it was two miles to Eureka. ☐

CHRIS But, in fact, it's three miles. ☐

TONY And she said the last bus left at nine o'clock. But it leaves at eight o'clock. ☐

CHRIS It's very strange. She said one night cost $13, but it costs $12. ☐

GRAMMAR

Reported speech: statements

You report what people said by using *said (that)* + clause. If the tense of the verb in the direct statement is the present simple, the tense of the verb in the reported statement is the past simple. Pronouns also change.

Direct statement	Reported statement
*"The last bus **leaves** at nine o'clock," she said.*	***She said that** the last bus **left** at nine o'clock.*
*"It**'s** two miles to Eureka," she said.*	***She said** it **was** two miles to Eureka.*

Other tenses

Other tenses "move back" in reported speech.

*"I just **started** work at the hostel," she said.*
***She said** she **had** just **started** work at the hostel.*
*"We**'re going** to Crescent City," he said.*
***He said** they **were going** to Crescent City.*
*"We**'ll stay** for just one night," he said*
***He said** they **would stay** for just one night.*

---

1. Write what the people actually said.

1. Tony said they were both sixteen.
2. The receptionist said it took an hour on foot.
3. She said there was a bus every hour.
4. She said there wasn't much to do at night.
5. Chris said they were exhausted.
6. He said they needed to go to bed early.

1. "We're both sixteen," said Tony.

2. Complete the rest of the conversation in *Listening and Reading* activity 4.

CHRIS And she said the bus _____ fifteen minutes. But in fact, it takes _____ minutes.

TONY And she said the hostel _____ at eleven A.M., but it _____ open all day.

CHRIS The brochure says that they _____ dinner from six to seven.

TONY But she said they were serving until eight o'clock. And she also said breakfast _____ at seven thirty…

CHRIS …when, in fact, it says here that breakfast _____ at seven.

TONY And she said that Fortuna _____ ten miles away, but it _____. It's eight miles away.

CHRIS And she said that Fortuna _____ north of here. But it _____ south of here!

3. 🔘 Listen and check.

VOCABULARY AND WRITING

1. Here are some new words from this lesson. Check that you know what they mean.

---
youth hostel   campsite   no smoking   hot tub   facilities charges   adult   travel   outdoor
---

2. Complete the letter Chris and Tony wrote to the manager of Redwoods Youth Hostel. Use as many of the words in the vocabulary box as possible.

E 5618 Freya Ave.
Portland, OR 62164

October 16, 1996

Sandy Donaldson
Manager
Youth Hostel Redwoods
Goldmine Avenue
Eureka, CA 90612

Dear Ms. Donaldson,

I wish to complain about the information your receptionist gave us when we stayed at the youth hostel. First of all, she said that one night cost $13 when in fact, it costs $12. Then she said that it was two...

GRAMMAR

> **Tense review**
>
> **There are five tenses presented in *Move Up* Elementary.**
>
> **Present simple**
> *I'm Polish. My name's Jan. What's your name?*
>
> **Present continuous**
> *You're **staying** with Mr. and Mrs. Hawkins. Mario **is** also **living** with them.*
>
> **Past simple**
> *A young man **arrived** at J.F.K. airport.*
> *His name **was** Jan Polanski.*
>
> **Present perfect**
> *I've **told** him we've finished.*
> *My parents **haven't met** many foreigners.*
>
> **Future simple**
> *I'll **see** you tomorrow.*
> *I'll **miss** you.*

1. Match the tenses 1–5 with their forms a–e below.

1. present simple
2. present continuous
3. past simple
4. present perfect
5. future simple

a. most regular verbs: infinitive + *-ed*
b. infinitive, or infinitive + *-s* for third person singular
c. *am/is/are* + present participle
d. *has/have* + past participle
e. *will* + infinitive

2. Write the name of the tenses in 1 by their uses below.

a. talking about something which began in the past and continues now
b. saying what is happening now or around now
c. making predictions
d. talking about present habits and routines
e. talking about finished actions in the past
f. talking about experiences
g. making decisions at the time of speaking

READING AND LISTENING

1. You're going to read a story called *Dear Jan… Love Ruth*, by Nick McIver. What type of story do you think it is?

– a love story   – a detective story   – science fiction
– a mystery

2. Work in pairs. Part 1 of the story is called *The Arrival*. Here are some words from part 1. Can you predict what happens?

Jan Polanski Poland language school New York stay family disco girls boyfriends stepped foot pretty name Ruth dance

3. Read part 1 and find out if you guessed correctly in 2.

The Arrival

A young man arrived at J.F.K. airport. His name was Jan Polanski and he came from Poland. He was in the United States for a course at an English language school. He took a cab to the Modern Language Institute, went inside, and met the director.

"Welcome to New York," the director said. "You're staying with the Hawkins family. Ah! Here's Mario. He's also living with them."

"Hello, Jan," said Mario.

That evening, after dinner Mario said, "Would you like to go dancing next Saturday?"

"Yes," said Jan. "Thanks very much."

On Saturday Jan went to Mario's room. He was feeling sick. "I can't go dancing tonight, Jan," said Mario. "But here's the address."

Jan arrived at the disco at nine o'clock. He liked dancing, but most of the girls were with their boyfriends. Suddenly a girl stepped on his foot.

"Oh," she said. "I'm sorry."

"That's all right," said Jan. He looked at the girl. She was very pretty.

"Can I buy you a drink?" asked Jan. They went to the bar.

"You're not American, are you?" said the girl.

"No," said Jan. "I'm Polish. My name's Jan. What's your name?"

"Ruth," she said. "Ruth Clark."

"Would you like to dance?" said Jan.

"Yes," said Ruth.

4. What do you think happens next? Work in pairs and guess the answers to these questions about part 2.

1. Will they see each other again?
2. Where do they go?
3. Who does Ruth see?
4. What does she tell him to do?
5. Do Ruth and Jan like each other?

5. Read part 2 and find the answers to the questions in 4.

Jan and Ruth

The next day, Jan met Ruth and they went for a walk in the park. Then they went to a coffee shop. Suddenly a tall man came over to the table.

"Jan, can you go outside?" said Ruth.

Jan waited outside for about ten minutes. Then the man came out and walked away.

"Who was that?" asked Jan.

"That was Bill. He was my boyfriend. I've told him we've finished. I don't like him any more." She looked into Jan's eyes. "Jan, I... like you... very much."

Jan smiled. "I like you very much too," he said.

6. Work in pairs. Part 3 is called *Ruth's Parents*. Here are some sentences from part 3 of the story. Decide who is speaking and who they are speaking to.

1. "How do you do, Mr. and Mrs. Clark…"
2. "Your parents don't like me very much."
3. "My parents haven't met many foreigners."
4. "Well, he didn't speak English very well."
5. "What's wrong with an American boyfriend?"
6. "But I don't like Bill any more…"
7. "…but I do like Jan. Maybe I love him."

 Now listen and check.

7. Work in pairs. Part 4 is called *Going Home*. Here are some phrases from part 4. What do you think happens next?

last day   goodbye   sad   come to Poland
living room   Bill was there   next morning
airport   I'll miss you   I love you   flight

8. Turn to Communication Activity 11 on page 52 and read part 4.

9. Work in pairs. Do you think the story has a happy or a sad ending? Talk about what will happen to Jan, Ruth… and Bill.

If you'd like to know the ending, turn to Communication Activity 16 on page 53.

VOCABULARY AND WRITING

1. Here are some words from the story. Check you remember what they mean.

language school   director   boyfriend   step
coffee shop   foreigner   strange   miss
forget   love   visitor

2. Write a paragraph describing a different ending to the story.

In December, Ruth bought a plane ticket to Poland…

Progress Check 16–20

VOCABULARY

1. You put a preposition after many verbs.

listen to   agree with   decide to   laugh at

Match the verbs and the prepositions. Use your dictionary if necessary.

Verbs – apologize   belong   complain   hear   insist
   pay   talk   think   worry

Prepositions – for   to   about   with   of   for
   on   in

2. Here are some of the topics in *Move Up* Elementary.

countries   jobs   family   furniture   entertainment
transportation   shops   food and drink
clothes   sports

Try to think of two words which go with each topic.

3. Work in pairs and compare your answers to 2.

GRAMMAR

1. Make decisions about the following situations.

1. There is nothing to eat.
2. You're very tired.
3. You don't feel well.
4. You can't remember what a word means.
5. You don't have any money.
6 You haven't spoken to your friend for a few days.

1. I'll go shopping.

2. Make predictions about the following things.

1. tomorrow's weather
2. traffic in your town
3. the next World Series
4. the next government of your country
5. your life in ten years
6. your English lessons

3. Rewrite these sentences in the passive.

1. Michelangelo painted the Sistine Chapel.
2. They grow cotton in Egypt.
3. They make Mercedes cars in Germany.
4. Hemingway wrote *The Old Man and the Sea*.
5. Verdi composed *Aida*.
6. The French built the Statue of Liberty.

4. Rewrite these sentences in reported speech.

1. "I'm sick," he said.
2. "It closes at seven," she said.
3. "It leaves in five minutes," she said.
4. "I work in an office," he said.
5. "We live in New York," they said.
6. "She goes shopping on Saturday," he said.

5. Write a sentence about yourself using each of these tenses.

1. present simple
2. present continuous
3. past simple
4. present perfect
5. future simple

SOUNDS

1. Say these words out loud. Is the underlined sound /ɔː/ or /ɔɪ/?

t<u>oy</u>   t<u>o</u>re   b<u>oy</u>   b<u>o</u>re   n<u>oi</u>se   s<u>o</u>re   d<u>oo</u>r   w<u>a</u>r
m<u>o</u>re

Listen and check. As you listen, say the words out loud.

2. Underline the stressed syllable in these words.

invent compose discover adult travel director foreigner forget

🔊 Listen and check. As you listen, say the words out loud.

3. 🔊 Listen and underline the words the speaker stresses.

> A young man arrived at J.F.K. airport. His name was Jan Polanski and he came from Poland. He was in the United States for a course at an English language school. He took a cab to the Modern Language Institute, went inside, and met the director.

Now read the passage out loud. Make sure you stress the same words.

SPEAKING

You're going to review the grammar and vocabulary you have learned in *Move Up* Elementary by playing *Move Up Snakes and Ladders*. Work in groups of three or four and follow the instructions.

Move Up Snakes and Ladders

1. Look at the game board on Communication Activity 1 on page 50.

2. Each player puts his/her counter on the square marked START and throws the dice.

3. The first player to throw a six starts.

4. Each player then throws the dice and moves his/her counter along the board according to the number thrown on the dice. As each player lands on a square, he/she has to answer the question on the square. (You can look back at the lesson to help you.) If a player answers the question correctly, he/she can remain on the square until their next turn. If a player answers a question incorrectly, he/she must go back 3 squares. The other players decide whether the answer given is right or wrong. If you land on a Progress Check square, the player on your left can ask you any question they like.

5. If you land on a ladder, you go up to the square shown and answer the question. If you land on a snake, you go down to the square shown and answer the question.

6. The winner is the first person to reach FINISH.

Communication Activities

Speaking

Now play *Move Up Snakes and Ladders.*

FINISH

Progress Check ?

40 Where's Jan staying? Have Ruth's parents met many foreigners?

39 Where is Jan from? Why is he in the United States?

38 What facilities does the youth hostel have?

37 When are the meals at the youth hostel?

36 Who wrote *Hamlet*? Name another play written by this person.

31 You need to get to New York quickly. What will you do?

32 Can you name three islands in the Caribbean? Have you ever been on a cruise?

33 What will the weather be like tomorrow?

34 Make a prediction for the future.

35 Where is coffee grown? What is grown in your country?

Progress Check ?

Progress Check ?

30 What were you good at in high school? *or* What places can you see and listen to English?

29 How did Trudy pass her exam? How does Antonia play the guitar?

28 What's your advice for a perfect day out?

27 What is your idea of a perfect day out?

26 How long have Ben and Abby been married? How long have you studied English?

21 What can you or can't you do in your English class?

22 What advice can you give to visitors to your country?

23 Have you ever been to San Francisco? Have you ever stayed in a hotel?

24 What is the most interesting place you have ever visited?

25 What is a deli? Would you like to visit New York?

Progress Check ?

Progress Check ?

20 What do you think is the most exciting sport? And the most dangerous sport?

19 What's your favorite sport?

18 Compare your country with another country?

17 Is Brazil smaller than the U.S.? Is your country colder than the U.S.?

16 What number do you call in a medical emergency? Why do you call this number?

11 Do you usually go shopping by yourself?

12 Name four things you buy as gifts for other people?

13 What does your friend look like? Describe him/her

14 What's Joan's purse made of? When did she lose it?

15 Name three parts of the body.

Progress Check ?

Progress Check ?

10 What is a *doggy bag*? What does a waitress do?

9 What would you like to eat? Do you like spaghetti?

8 What's Andrea going to do in the New Year? What's your New Year's resolution?

7 What are you going to do this weekend?

6 Name four items of clothing.

1 What is the name of Agatha Christie's famous detective?

2 Why did Agatha Christie disappear?

3 When is New Year's Day? When is your birthday?

4 How do you say *July 10* and *October 31*?

5 What's Erin doing? What are you wearing?

Progress Check ?

START

2 *Lesson 2*

Speaking, activity 2

Pair A: Rewrite these facts as quiz questions.

1. The Kobe earthquake was in 1995.
2. Martin Luther King died in 1968.
3. Alexander Graham Bell invented the telephone.
4. Michelangelo was 88 years old when he died.
5. Joseph Stalin was born in Georgia.

1. When was the Kobe earthquake?

Now continue the quiz with Pair B. Ask and answer each other's questions.

3 *Lesson 1*

Grammar, activity 3

Write five statements about your past, three true and two false.

I was born in Belgium. I married Hercule Poirot.

Now work in pairs. Show your statements to your partner. Your partner must try to guess which are the false statements.

You didn't marry Hercule Poirot!

Now turn back to page 3.

4 *Lesson 1*

Vocabulary and Reading, activity 5

Student A: Ask Student B these questions. Answer his/her questions in turn.

1. Why was Agatha Christie famous?
2. What was the final mystery?
3. When was she born?
4. Where did she live?
5. Who did she marry in 1914?

Now turn back to page 3.

5 *Lesson 16*

Reading and Speaking, activity 3

Student B: You want to know more about the Caribbean Cruise. Ask Student A, who is the travel agent, the following questions and then make a decision:

Will there be a guided tour on Curaçao?
Will we be able to visit both Trinidad and Tobago?
Will there be two twin beds or one queen size bed in the double suites on *The Seaworthy?*

With Student C, decide what to do.

6 *Lesson 8*

Functions and Grammar, activity 3

Student A: Listen to Student B and say what he/she *should/shouldn't* do.

Now act out these situations with Student B. Listen to his/her advice.

– you feel sick
– you feel unhappy all the time
– you are hungry
– you don't like your job

Now turn back to page 18.

7 *Lesson 3*

Vocabulary and Listening, activity 1

Look at the picture for different items of clothing and check that you know what the words mean.

jacket   sweater

skirt

socks   shoes   shorts

Now turn back to page 6.

8 *Lesson 1*

Vocabulary and Reading, activity 5

Student B: Ask Student A these questions. Answer his/her questions in turn.

1. When did she write her first story?
2. What did she do in December 1926?
3. What did everyone think?
4. Where did her husband find her?
5. Who did she marry in 1930?

Now turn back to page 3.

9 *Lesson 8*

Functions and Grammar, activity 3

Student B: Act out these situations with Student A and listen to his/her advice.

– you don't get enough exercise

– you feel tired all the time

– you are thirsty

– you have a headache

Now listen to Student A and say what he/she *should/shouldn't* do.

Now turn back to page 18.

10 *Lesson 16*

Reading and Speaking, activity 3

Student A: You're a travel agent. Student B and C want to know more about the Caribbean Cruise. Read the information below and answer their questions.

All flights are economy class or business class, but business class is extra.
There will be a personal guided tour on Curaçao or a large-group tour.
They will be able to visit *either* Trinidad *or* Tobago.
There will be two twin beds *or* one queen size bed in the double suites on *The Seaworthy*.
They will stay in a hotel on Trinidad (extra) or on *The Seaworthy* on days 6 and 7.
They will be able to explore Barbados *or* have a scuba diving lesson.

Ask them to make a decision.

11 *Lesson 20*

Reading and Listening, activity 8. Part 4

Going Home

It was the last day of the course at the Modern Language Institute and Jan was very sad. He said goodbye to Mario and his other friends and left the school. That night, Jan and Ruth went for a long walk in the park.

"I love you, Ruth," Jan said.

"I love you too, Jan."

"I'm going home tomorrow. But why don't you come to Poland at Christmas?" said Jan.

"Yes," said Ruth. "I'd love to."

Jan suddenly laughed. "I'm going to see you again!"

Ruth got home at eleven o'clock that evening. She went into the house and her mother met her in the hall.

"You have a visitor, Ruth," she said.

Ruth went into the living room. Bill was there.

The next morning, Ruth went to the airport with Jan.

Jan said, "It's September now. And you're coming to Poland in December."

"I know," said Ruth. "But I'll miss you."

At that moment, they called Jan's flight.

"Goodbye, Ruth," said Jan. "I love you."

"Goodbye, Jan. Write to me."

"Yes, of course."

Ruth drove away from the airport. She went to the park and thought about Jan.

Now turn back to page 47.

12 *Lesson 16*

Reading and Speaking, activity 3

Student C: You want to know more about the Caribbean Cruise. Ask Student A, who is the travel agent, the following questions and then make a decision:

Will the flight from Miami be business class or economy class?

Where will we stay on days 6 and 7?

Will we be able to explore and have a scuba diving lesson on Barbados?

With Student B, decide what to do.

13 *Lesson 2*

Speaking, activity 2

Pair B: Rewrite these facts as quiz questions.

1. The Mexico City earthquake was in 1984.
2. Yuri Gagarin was the first man in space.
3. The first American walked on the moon in 1969.
4. King Henry VIII of England and Wales had six wives.
5. Sigmund Freud was born in Vienna.

1. *When was the Mexico City earthquake?*

Now continue the quiz with Pair A. Ask and answer each other's questions.

14 *Lesson 10*

Vocabulary and Listening, activity 1

Look at the pictures of different sports and check you know what they are.

15 *Lesson 3*

Reading and Speaking, activity 3

Add up your scores using the following table. Then look at the profiles below to find out what your clothes say about you.

1. a. 2	b. 3	c. 1	**6.** a. 3	b. 2	c. 1
2. a. 2	b. 3	c. 1	**7.** a. 3	b. 2	c. 1
3. a. 2	b. 1	c. 3	**8.** a. 2	b. 1	c. 3
4. a. 2	b. 1	c. 3	**9.** a. 1	b. 3	c. 2
5. a. 3	b. 2	c. 1	**10.** a. 1	b. 2	c. 3

21–30 points. You like to wear exactly what you want. Sometimes this may get you into trouble.

11–20 points. You are quite casual. Sometimes you don't wear the right clothes for the situation.

1–10 points. You're very careful to wear the right clothes for the right situation.

16 *Lesson 20*

**Reading and Listening, activity 9.
Part 5**

The End

Jan wrote several letters to Ruth. But every time Mrs. Clark found the letters she burned them. Ruth was very sad. She thought, Jan doesn't love me any more. He's forgotten about me.

Bill was very kind to Ruth at this time. At the end of November, Ruth went to a party with Bill.

Now turn back to page 47.

Grammar Review

CONTENTS

Present simple	54
Present continuous	55
Past simple	56
Future simple (will)	56
Present perfect simple	57
Questions	57
Imperatives	58
Verb patterns	58
Going to	58
Have to (for obligation)	58
Modal verbs	58
Pronouns	59
Articles	59
Plurals	59
Possessives	60
Expressions of quantity	
Countable and uncountable nouns	60
Some and any	60
Adjectives	
Position of adjectives	60
Comparative and superlative adjectives	60
Adverbs	
Formation of adverbs	60
Position of adverbs of frequency	61
Prepositions of time and place	61
Present simple passive	61
Reported speech	61

Present simple

Form

You use the contracted form in spoken and informal written English.

Be

Affirmative	Negative
I'm (I am)	I'm not (am not)
you	you
we 're (are)	we aren't (are not)
they	they
he	he
she 's (is)	she isn't (is not)
it	it

Questions	Short answers
Am I?	Yes, I am.
	No, I'm not.
Are you/we/they?	Yes, you/we/they are.
	No, you/we/they're not.
Is he/she/it?	Yes, he/she/it is.
	No, he/she/it isn't.

Have

Affirmative	Negative
I	I
you have	you haven't (have not)
we	we
they	they
he	he
she has	she hasn't (has not)
it	it

Questions	Short answers
Have I/you/we/they?	Yes, I/you/we/they have.
	No, I/you/we/they haven't.
Has he/she/it?	Yes, he/she/it has.
	No, he/she/it hasn't.

Regular verbs

Affirmative		Negative	
I		I	
you	work	you	don't (do not) work
we		we	
they		they	
he		he	
she	works	she	doesn't (does not) work
it		it	

Questions	Short answers
Do I/you/we/they work?	Yes, I/you/we/they do.
	No, I/you/we/they don't (do not).
Does he/she/it work?	Yes, he/she/it does.
	No, he/she/it doesn't (does not).

Question words with *is/are*

What's your name?   Where are your parents?

Question words with *does/do*

Where does he live?   What do you do?

Present simple: third person singular

You add -*s* to most verbs.

takes, gets

You add -*es* to *do, go* and verbs which end in -*ch, -ss, -sh,* and -*x.*

does, goes, watches, finishes, fixes

You drop the -*y* and add -*ies* to verbs ending in -*y.*

carries, tries

Use

You use the present simple:

- to talk about customs. (See Book A, Lesson 7.)
  In Mexico people have dinner at ten or eleven in the evening.
  In the United States people leave work at five in the afternoon.

- to talk about habits and routines. (See Book A, Lesson 9.)
  I go running every day.
  We see friends on the weekend.

- to say how often you do things. (See Book A, Lesson 11.)
  I always get up at seven o'clock.
  I sometimes go shopping in the evening.

- to describe something that is true for a long time. (See Book B, Lesson 3.)
  He wears glasses.

Present continuous

Form

You form the present continuous with *be* + present participle (-*ing*). You use the contracted form in spoken and informal written English.

Affirmative		Negative	
I'm (am) working		I'm not (am not) working	
you		you	
we	're (are) working	we	aren't (are not) working
they		they	
he		he	
she	's (is) working	she	isn't (is not) working
it		it	

Questions	Short answers
Am I working?	Yes, I am.
	No, I'm not.
Are you/we/they working?	Yes, you/we/they are.
	No, you/we/they aren't.
Is he/she/it working?	Yes, he/she/it is.
	No, he/she/it isn't.

Question words

What are you doing?   Why are you laughing?

Present participle (-*ing*) endings

You form the present participle of most verbs by adding -*ing*:

go – going   visit – visiting

You drop the final -*e* and add -*ing* to verbs ending in -*e*.

make – making   have – having

You double the final consonant of verbs of one syllable ending in a single vowel and a consonant and add -*ing*.

get – getting   shop – shopping

You add -*ing* to verbs ending in a vowel and -*y* or -*w*.

draw – drawing   play – playing

You don't usually use these verbs in the continuous form.

believe feel hate hear know like love see smell sound taste think understand want

Use

You use the present continuous:

- to describe something that is happening now or around now. (See Book A, Lesson 15 and Book B, Lesson 3.)
  We're flying at 30,000 feet.
  She's wearing a yellow dress.

Past simple

Form
You use the contracted form in spoken and informal written English.

Be

Affirmative	Negative
I	I
he was	he wasn't (was not)
she	she
it	it
you	you
we were	we weren't (were not)
they	they

Have

Affirmative	Negative
I	I
you	you
we	we
they had	they didn't (did not) have
he	he
she	she
it	it

Regular verbs

Affirmative	Negative
I	I
you	you
we	we
they worked	they didn't (did not) work
he	he
she	she
it	it

Questions	Short answers
Did I/you/we/they work?	Yes, I/you/we/they did.
he/she/it	he/she/it
	No, I/you/we/they didn't.
	he/she/it

Question words
What did you do yesterday?   *Why did you leave?*

Past simple endings

You add -*ed* to most regular verbs.
walk – walked   watch – watched

You add -*d* to verbs ending in -*e*.
close – closed   continue – continued

You double the consonant and add -*ed* to verbs of one syllable ending in a single vowel and a consonant.
stop – stopped   plan – planned

You drop the -*y* and add -*ied* to verbs ending in -*y*.
study – studied   try – tried

You add -*ed* to verbs ending in a vowel + -*y*.
play – played   annoy – annoyed

Pronunciation of past simple endings

/t/ *finished, liked, walked*
/d/ *continued, lived, stayed*
/ɪd/ *decided, started, visited*

Expressions of past time
(See Book B, Lesson 2.)

yesterday morning/afternoon/evening
last Saturday/week/month/year
two weeks ago/six months ago

Use
You use the past simple:

● to talk about an action or event in the past that is finished.
(See Book A, Lessons 16, 18, and 20, and Book B, Lesson 2.)
What were you like as a child?
I started learning English last year.
Did they go to Hong Kong last year?

Future simple (*will*)

Form
You form the future simple with *will* + infinitive. You use the contracted form in spoken and informal written English.

Affirmative	Negative
I	I
you	you
we	we
they 'll (will) work	they won't (will not) work
he	he
she	she
it	it

Questions	Short answers
Will I/you/we/they work?	Yes, I/you/we/they will.
he/she/it/	he/she/it/
	No, I/you/we/they won't.
	he/she/it/

Question words
What will you do?   *Where will you go?*

Use

You use the future simple:

- to talk about a decision you make at the moment of speaking. (See Book B, Lessons 6 and 16.)
  I'll take the blue T-shirt.
  I think I'll go out tonight.
  I'll call back later.

- to make a prediction or express an opinion about the future. (See Book B, Lesson 17.)
  There'll be more and more people in the world.
  I think it'll be hot tomorrow.

Present perfect simple

Form

You form the present perfect simple with *has/have* + past participle. You use the contracted form in spoken and informal written English.

Affirmative		Negative	
I		I	
you	've (have) worked	you	haven't (have not) worked
we		we	
they		they	
he		he	
she	's (has) worked	she	hasn't (has not) worked
it		it	

Questions	Short answers
Have I/you/we/they worked?	Yes, I/you/we/they have.
	No, I/you/we/they haven't.
Has he/she/it worked?	Yes, he/she/it has.
	No, he/she/it hasn't.

Past participles

All regular and some irregular verbs have past participles which are the same as their past simple form.
Regular: *move – moved, finish – finished, visit – visited*
Irregular: *leave – left, find – found, buy – bought*

Some irregular verbs have past participles which are not the same as the past simple form.
go – went – gone   be – was/were – been
drink – drank – drunk   ring – rang – rung

Use

You use the present perfect simple:

- to talk about past experiences. You often use it with *ever* and *never*. (See Book B, Lesson 12.)
  Have you ever stayed in a hotel? (=Do you have the experience of staying in a hotel?)
  Yes, I have. (=Yes, I have stayed in a hotel at some point, but it's not important when.)
  No, I've never stayed in a hotel.

  Remember that if you ask for and give more information about these experiences, actions, or states, such as *when, how, why,* and *how long,* you use the past simple.
  When did you stay in a hotel?   When I was in France last year.

- to talk about something that started in the past and continues now. (see Book B, Lesson 13.)
  I've lived in New York all my life.
  We've been married for fifty years.

  You use *for* to talk about the duration of the action (how long it has continued).
  I've been here for fifty-one years.

  You use *since* to talk about when the action started.
  We've lived here since we got married.
  I've worked here since 1946.

  Remember, you use the past simple if you are talking about a finished action in the past.
  I started working here in 1946.

Questions

You can form questions in two ways:

- without a question word. (See Book A, Lesson 3.)
  Are you American?
  Was he born in Japan?
  Do you have any brothers?
  Did you get up late this morning?

- with a question word such as *who, what, where, when, how,* and *why.* (See Book A, Lesson 9.)
  What's his job?
  How old is he?
  What do you do to relax?
  Where were you born?

You can put a noun after *what* and *which.*
What time is it?   Which road will you take?

You can put an adjective or an adverb after *how.*
How much is it?   How long does it take by car?
How fast can you drive?

You can use *who, what,* or *which* as pronouns to ask about the subject of the sentence. You don't use *do* or *did.*
What's your first name?   Who was Agatha Christie?

You can use *who, what,* or *which* as pronouns to ask about the object of the sentence. You use *do* or *did.*
What did Agatha Christie do?   Who did she marry?

You can form more indirect, polite questions with one of the following question phrases.
Can I help you?
Could I have some water, please?
Would you like a regular or a large soda?

Imperatives

The imperative has exactly the same form as the infinitive (without *to*) and does not usually have a subject. You use the imperative:

- to give directions. (See Book A, Lesson 14.)
  Go along Lincoln Street.
  Turn left on Washington Street.

- to give instructions and advice. (See Book B, Lesson 14.)
  Come in.
  Sit down.
  Check the weather forecast before you go.

You use *don't* + imperative to give a negative instruction.
Don't take too much to carry.

Verb patterns

There are several possible patterns after certain verbs which involve *-ing* form verbs and infinitive constructions with or without *to.*

-ing form verbs

You can put an *-ing* form verb after certain verbs.
(See Book A, Lesson 10.)
I like playing soccer on the beach.
Pete hates traveling by plane.

Remember that *would like to do something* refers to an activity at a specific time in the future.
I'd like to go to a movie next Saturday.

When you *like doing something,* this is something you enjoy all the time.
I like going to the movies. I go most weekends.

to + infinitive

You can put *to* + infinitive after many verbs.
Here are some of them:
decide go have hope learn like need want
He decided to go to Mexico for a vacation.

Use
You use *to* + infinitive (the infinitive of purpose):

- to say why people do things. (See Book B, Lesson 14.)
  You go to a drugstore to buy sunscreen.
  You go to the bus stop to catch a bus.

- to describe the purpose of something.
  (See Book B, Lesson 14.)
  You use ice to keep things cold.

Going to

You use *going to* + infinitive:

- to talk about future intentions or plans which are fairly certain. (See Book B, Lesson 4.)
  I'm going to see my friends more often.

- to talk about something that we can see now is sure to happen in the future. (See Book B, Lesson 4.)
  She's going to have a baby.

Have to (obligation)

You use *have to* + infinitive to talk about something you're obliged to do. (See Book B, Lesson 11.)
I have to go to work tomorrow.
Remember, *don't have to* means you are not obliged to do something:
Women don't have to cover their heads (= It is not necessary for women to cover their heads.)

Modal verbs

The following verbs are modal verbs.
can could should will would

Form
Modal verbs:

- have the same form for all persons.
  I should go.   He should be quiet.

- don't take the auxiliary *do* in questions and negatives.
  Can you use a computer?
  You shouldn't be late for the meeting.

- take an infinitive without *to.*
  I can type.
  You should see a doctor.

Use
You use *can*:

- to talk about general ability, something you are able to do on most occasions. (See Book A, Lesson 13.)
  I can play the piano.
  I can drive a car.

- to ask for permission. (See Book B, Lesson 6.)
  Can I try this on?

- to say if you're allowed to do something.
  (See Book B, Lesson 11.)
  You can kiss in public.

You can also use *could*. *Can* is a little less formal than *could*.

You use *could*:

- to ask for something politely.
  Could I have some water, please?

- to ask people to do things
  Could you tell me your name?

- to ask for permission
  Could I try this on?

You use *should*:

- to give less strong advice. It can also express a mild
  obligation or the opinion of the speaker.
  (See Book B, Lesson 8.)
  You should go to bed.
  You shouldn't go to work.

For uses of *will* see Future simple (*will*).

You use *would like* + noun or *would like to* + infinitive:

- to offer or request something politely.
  (See Book B, Lesson 5.)
  Would you like a drink?
  What would you like to drink?
  I'd like a cheeseburger, please.
  I'd like to go to a movie tonight.

Remember that you use *like* to say what you like all the time.
I like Coke. (= always)
I'd like a Coke. (= now)

Pronouns

Subject	Object	Possessive
(See Book A, Lesson 10.)	(See Book A, Lesson 10.)	(See Book B, Lesson 7.)
I	me	mine
you	you	yours
he	him	his
she	her	hers
it	it	its
we	us	ours
they	them	theirs

Articles

There are many rules for the use of articles. Here are some
of the most useful. (See Book A, Lessons 2 and 12.)
You use the indefinite article (*a/an*):

- to talk about something for the first time.
  He works in an office in Seattle.
  I get a train to work.

- with jobs.
  He's an accountant.
  He's a flight attendant.

- with certain expressions of quantity.
  I go to a movie once or twice a month.
  There are several trains a day.

You use *an* for nouns which begin with a vowel.
an accountant, an apple

You use the definite article (*the*):

- to talk about something again.
  The office is in the center of town.

- when there is only one.
  the sky
  the sun

Before vowels you pronounce *the* /ðiː/.

You don't use any article:

- with certain expressions.
  by train   by plane   at work   at home

- with most countries, meals, languages.
  She often goes to Disneyland.
  She lives in Ohio.
  Let's have lunch.
  I speak Russian.

Plurals

You form the plural of most nouns with *-s*.
(See Book A, Lessons 4 and 6.)
bag – bags, book – books, key – keys

For nouns which end in *-y*, you drop *-y* and add *-ies*.
diary – diaries, baby – babies

You add *-es* to nouns which end in *-o, -ch, -ss, -sh,* and *-x*.
watch – watches, glass – glasses

There are some irregular plurals.
man – men, woman – women, child – children

Possessives

Possessive 's

You add *'s* to singular nouns to show possession.
(See Book A, Lesson 6.)
John's mother.   His teacher's book.

You add *s'* to regular plural nouns.
My parents' names are Jorge and Pilar.
The boys' room.

You add *'s* to irregular plural nouns.
Their children's names are Pedro and Tomás.
The men's room.

Possessive adjectives

You can find the main uses for possessive adjectives in Book A, Lesson 2.

Form						
I	you	he	she	it	we	they
my	your	his	her	its	our	their

Whose

You use *whose* to ask who something belongs to.
(See Lesson 7.)
Whose bag is this?
Whose are these shoes?

Expressions of quantity

Countable and uncountable nouns

Countable nouns have both a singular and a plural form.
(See Book A, Lesson 17.)
a banana – bananas, a tomato – tomatoes

Uncountable nouns do not usually have a plural form.
water, juice, wine

If you talk about different kinds of uncountable nouns, they become countable.
Budweiser and Coors are both American beers.

Some and any

You usually use *some* with plural and uncountable nouns in affirmative sentences when you are not interested in the exact number. (See Book A, Lessons 8 and 17.)
We need some fruit and vegetables.

You usually use *any* with plural and uncountable nouns in negative sentences and questions.
(See Book A, Lessons 8 and 17.)
We don't have any carrots.
Do we have any milk?

You use *some* in questions when you ask for, offer or suggest something.
How about some oranges?

Adjectives

Position of adjectives

You can put an adjective in two positions.
(See Book A, Lesson 4.)

- after the verb *to be*.
  The book is very interesting.

- before a noun.
  It's an interesting book.

Comparative and superlative adjectives

Form

You add *-er* to most adjectives for the comparative form, and *-est* for the superlative form. (See Book B, Lessons 9 and 10.)
cold – colder – coldest   cheap – cheaper – cheapest

You add *-r* to adjectives ending in *-e* for the comparative form, and *-st* for the superlative form.
large – larger – largest   fine – finer – finest

You drop the *-y* and add *-ier* to adjectives ending in *-y* for the comparative form, and *-iest* for the superlative form.
happy – happier – happiest   friendly – friendlier – friendliest

You double the final consonant and add *-er* or *-est* to adjectives of one syllable ending in a vowel and a consonant.
hot – hotter – hottest   thin – thinner – thinnest

You use *more* for the comparative form and *most* for the superlative form of longer adjectives.
expensive – more expensive – most expensive
important – more important – most important

Some adjectives have irregular comparative and superlative forms.
good – better – best   bad – worse – worst

With the superlative form you usually use *the* before the adjective in its superlative form.
James is the tallest person in the room.

You use a comparative + *than* when you compare two things which are different.
Brazil is bigger than the United States.

Adverbs

Formation of adverbs

You use an adverb to describe a verb.
(See Book B, Lesson 15.)
She speaks English fluently.
He drives carelessly.

You form an adverb by adding *-ly* to the adjective.
fluent – fluently   careless – carelessly

If the adjective ends in *-y,* you drop the *-y* and add *-ily.*
happy – happily   easy – easily

Some adverbs have the same form as the adjective they come from.
late, early, hard, fast

The adverb from the adjective *good* is *well.*
She's a good writer.   *She writes well.*

Position of adverbs of frequency

You usually put adverbs of frequency before the verb.
(See Book A, Lesson 11.)
I always get up at seven o'clock.
I often have a drink with friends.

But you put them after the verb *to be.*
I'm never late for work.

Prepositions of time and place

in, at, on, to

You use *in*:
- with seasons and months of the year.
  in winter, in September, in March
- with places. (See Book A, Lesson 5.)
  in the classroom, in the photograph, in Ecuador
- with times of the day. (See Book A, Lesson 7.)
  in the morning, in the afternoon

You use *at*:
- with certain expressions. (See Book A, Lesson 11.)
  at school, at home, at work
- with times of the day. (See Book A, Lesson 11.)
  at night, at seven o'clock

You use *on*:
- with days and dates. (See Book A, Lesson 11.)
  on Sunday, on Monday morning, on June 15,
  on the weekend

You use *to*:
- with places.
  Bridget goes to Florida every month.

You use *from... to*:
- to express how long something lasts.
  (See Book A, Lesson 11.)
  The store is open from seven to nine o'clock.

Present simple passive

You form the present simple passive with *am/is/are* + past participle. (See Book B, Lesson 18.)
Honda cars are made in Japan.

Use
You use the passive to focus on the object of the sentence.
This palace was built by Palladio in 1635.

Reported speech

Statements

You report what people said by using *said that* + clause. Notice how the tense of the verb in the direct statement moves one tense back in the reported statement.
(See Book B, Lesson 19.)

Direct statement	**Reported statement**
"The movie ends at ten o'clock," she said.	*She said the movie ended at ten o'clock.*
"We're going on vacation next year," she said	*She said they were going on vacation next year.*
"We'll catch the bus downtown," he said.	*He said they would catch the bus downtown.*
"I watched TV all evening," he said.	*He said he had watched TV all evening.*

Tapescripts

Lesson 2   Listening and Speaking, activity 2

SPEAKER 1 Oh, it was five months ago, in August, we were talking about it yesterday evening. It was a pretty typical wedding day, starting with the excitement of getting dressed in my wedding dress. Then we drove to the church, and we arrived about five minutes late, as is traditional. Then the service started and after the service, there was a photographer. And finally we went to the wedding reception, which was wonderful, and we danced until about three in the morning. It was a wonderful day.

SPEAKER 2 It was last Thursday when I got my A.P. exam results. After a year of hard work, at the end of the year, the school year, that is, finally the day arrived when I found out if I had passed the exam. I woke up early and went down to the building where they put up the exam results on lists. The building was closed so I waited about ten minutes with a bunch of other students. Then they opened the doors and we went in, and I found my name on the list. I'd passed! What a great feeling! I left the building, dancing and singing, people probably thought I was crazy.

SPEAKER 3 It was in 1987, on December eleventh, that my parents had their golden wedding anniversary, that's fifty years of marriage. And we had a big party for them, all my brothers and sisters, all the grandchildren, nephews, nieces, friends, and neighbors, there were about sixty people in all. We worked all day from nine to five preparing the food and decorating the house. And the funny thing was—they didn't know about the party until they got home. They walked in the door and everyone started singing. It was a great surprise!

Lesson 3   Vocabulary and Listening, activity 4

MAN Hey, this is a great party.
WOMAN I'm glad you were able to come.
MAN Could you introduce me to your friends? Which one is Erin? I've heard so much about her.
WOMAN Well, can you see the woman by the door?
MAN Ah, which one?
WOMAN The one in the jeans.
MAN No, which door?
WOMAN There is only one door.
MAN Oh, right! Yes, I see. The one in the jeans and the T-shirt.
WOMAN Yes, she's standing by the door and talking to a friend. She's smiling at him.
MAN Great smile. And ah, what about John?
WOMAN John is sitting down in the armchair by the window.
MAN Is he the one wearing the sweater and pants?
WOMAN No, John's wearing the shirt and tie.
MAN OK, I see him. Nice tie. Love that yellow.
WOMAN And Ed is the man over by the window. He's laughing at something. Probably laughing at John's tie.
MAN The man in the sneakers with the blue shirt and black jeans?
WOMAN That's Ed!
MAN Right! And Louise?
WOMAN Louise is standing by the TV. She's wearing a black dress.
MAN Yes, I can see her. Hey, she's smiling at me.
WOMAN She smiles at everyone. She wears glasses, but um, she doesn't have them on right now.
MAN No, I'm sure she's smiling at me…

Lesson 4   Reading and Listening, activity 3

Speaker 1
MAN Well, our jobs take up a lot of our time, and when the weekend comes, we're very tired.
WOMAN But the trouble is, we don't have any social life now.
MAN So, our New Year's Resolution is we're going to invite more friends for dinner.
WOMAN Yes, because we don't entertain much. And we'd like people to invite us, too.

Speaker 2
MAN I'm taking a year off before I go to school, and I don't know much about foreign countries, so I'm going to travel around Europe with my girlfriend. Our grandparents were from Europe, so we both want to visit… you know… to find our roots.

Speaker 3
WOMAN I spend my life driving to school, teaching, and then coming home. So I'm going to get in shape because I don't get enough exercise. I'm going to start running when I get home in the evening.

Speaker 4
MAN We have a family now, and we need more space for all the stuff that kids need. Our resolution is that we're going to move.
WOMAN Yes, because our house is too small for four people. The trouble is, we still like it here, though.
MAN Yes, it's going to be hard to leave this house.

Lesson 5   Vocabulary and Listening, activity 4

CASHIER Good afternoon. May I help you?
CUSTOMER Good afternoon. Yes, I'd like a cheeseburger with fries and an orange soda, please.
CASHIER Would you like a regular or a large soda?
CUSTOMER Regular.
CASHIER Would you like anything else?
CUSTOMER Yes, I'd like some ice cream, please.
CASHIER What flavor would you like?
CUSTOMER Strawberry, please.
CASHIER OK.
CUSTOMER How much is that?
CASHIER That's six dollars and forty-nine cents, please.
CUSTOMER Here you are.
CASHIER Thank you.

Lesson 6   Speaking and Listening, activity 4

CLERK May I help you?
CUSTOMER Yes, I'm looking for a sweater.
CLERK We have some sweaters over here. What color are you looking for?
CUSTOMER This blue one is nice.
CLERK Yes, it is. Is it for you?
CUSTOMER Yes. Can I try it on?
CLERK Yes, go ahead.
CUSTOMER No, it's too small. It doesn't fit me. Do you have one in a bigger size?
CLERK No, I'm afraid not. What about the red one?
CUSTOMER No, I don't like the color. Red doesn't look good on me. OK, I'll leave it. Thank you.
CLERK Goodbye.

Lesson 7   Listening and Speaking, activity 2

OFFICIAL Good afternoon, how can I help you?
CUSTOMER I lost my bag. I put it down somewhere in Disneyland, and forgot about it.
OFFICIAL Well, don't worry, ma'am, it'll show up. I'll just take down some details. Could you tell me your name, please?
CUSTOMER Yes, my name's Jill Fairfield.
OFFICIAL Jill Fairfield. Is that Mrs. Fairfield?
CUSTOMER Ms. Fairfield.
OFFICIAL OK, and your address?
CUSTOMER 11510 North Nevada, Springdale, Washington 92704.
OFFICIAL Springdale, Washington 92704. OK, and your telephone number?
CUSTOMER 509 555-6473.
OFFICIAL Right, and you say it was a bag that you lost?
CUSTOMER That's right.
OFFICIAL And you lost it in Disneyland?
CUSTOMER That's correct. At about eleven in the morning.
OFFICIAL And that was today, right?
CUSTOMER Yes.
OFFICIAL So, Thursday July twenty-first. And can you describe it to me?
CUSTOMER Well, it was large, square, and it was made of black nylon.
OFFICIAL And was there anything in it?
CUSTOMER Yes, there was my purse, a calculator, an address book, a newspaper, and a comb.
OFFICIAL Was there any money in the purse?
CUSTOMER No, well, maybe a couple of dollars.
OFFICIAL Well, we will let you know as soon as we find it.
CUSTOMER Thank you so much.

Lesson 8   Vocabulary and Listening, activity 2

Conversation 1

DOCTOR Good morning. How are you?
PATIENT Fine, thanks.
DOCTOR So, if you're fine, why are you here to see me?
PATIENT No, what I meant was, oh, never mind. I have a headache. I seem to have it all the time.
DOCTOR I see. Any other symptoms?
PATIENT Well, I have a cough, too.
DOCTOR Do you smoke?
PATIENT Yes I do. And I feel tired all the time.
DOCTOR OK, let's take a look.

Conversation 2

DOCTOR And what seems to be the matter?
PATIENT I feel sick and I have a stomachache.
DOCTOR Let me see. Do you have a headache?
PATIENT Yes, I do.
DOCTOR You look pretty hot. Yes, you have a slight temperature. I think it might be something you ate yesterday.
PATIENT I only had a sandwich yesterday.
DOCTOR What kind of sandwich?
PATIENT It was a cheese sandwich.
DOCTOR Well, it's probably nothing serious, but I'll give you some medicine…

Conversation 3

DOCTOR So, what's up?
PATIENT I hurt my leg.
DOCTOR How did you do that?
PATIENT In a football game.
DOCTOR Football! Don't you think you're a little old to play football?
PATIENT Well, I'm only seventy-three.
DOCTOR Really! Well, let me see now…

Lesson 9   Reading and Listening, activity 2

Q Karl, tell me something about Sweden. Is it a large country?
KARL Yes, it is pretty large, at least for a country in Europe. It's about 170,000 square miles.
Q 170,000. Hmm… about the size of California then… And what's the coldest month? January, I suppose?
KARL Yes, January is really cold. The temperature is about minus three degrees Celsius.
Q That's about 27° Fahrenheit, right? And how hot is it in the summer?
KARL Actually, it gets pretty warm. In July, the average temperature is eighteen degrees Celsius—that's 64° Fahrenheit or so.
Q And what's the average rainfall?
KARL Well, for Sweden, it's 22 inches, but it's less in Stockholm.
Q And what's the population?
KARL There are over eight and a half million people. Not so many for such a large country.
Q And what about the armed services? How many troops are there?
KARL We only have about 65,000 soldiers.
Q 65,000, I see. And when do children start school?
KARL They start at the age of seven and continue for ten years, until they're seventeen.
Q Ten years.
KARL Of course, some students go on to university.

Lesson 10   Vocabulary and Listening, activity 5

KATY What's your favorite sport, Andy?
ANDY Well, I like most sports, but I suppose I like baseball most of all. Like most people.
KATY Yes, I suppose baseball is the most popular sport. Personally, I don't like baseball. I don't enjoy competitive sports. I like cycling and horseback riding.
ANDY Isn't horseback riding really expensive?
KATY Yes, it's more expensive than cycling.
ANDY I think horseback riding is the most expensive sport. What do you think is the most tiring sport?
KATY Well, horseback riding is very tiring.
ANDY Do you think it's more tiring than, say, swimming?
KATY Oh, yes, I'm exhausted after I've been riding. What about you?
ANDY Well, for me swimming is the most tiring. What do you think is the most dangerous sport?
KATY I think hang gliding is very dangerous.
ANDY Well, that's what many people think. But you know, there are more accidents caused by windsurfing than there are with hang gliding.
KATY Is that a fact? Which is the most difficult sport, in your opinion?
ANDY How about climbing? I think climbing is very hard.
KATY Well, I think skiing is more difficult than climbing.
ANDY No, I don't agree. Climbing looks incredibly hard.
KATY And what do you think is the most exciting sport?
ANDY Well, baseball, I think. What about you?
KATY It has to be auto racing. Auto racing is the most exciting sport for me.

Lesson 11   Listening, activity 1

JAMES Well, in Australia, you don't have to ask if you want to take a photograph of someone you don't know. Even someone you do know will not usually mind if you take a picture.
Yes, I've heard about this custom with shoes in Japan. Actually, it's quite a good idea. But you don't have to take your shoes off when you go into someone's house in Australia, unless of course, they're very dirty. I usually change my shoes when I get home, but I don't take them off when I visit people.
And women don't have to cover their heads in Australia, most of the time. Sometimes, in certain churches, women wear a hat or a scarf on their heads, but they don't have to do that in the street or at work.
Pointing at people, yes, that's true in Australia, you shouldn't point at people. If you do, people think you're rather rude. It's the same in America, I think.

In Australia you can look people in the eye, though. It shows you're interested in them and what they're saying. It's a sign of politeness. But you shouldn't look people in the eye for long, 'cause they begin to feel uncomfortable.

Well, you *can* kiss in public in Australia, but not many people do. We're fairly relaxed in my country, so almost anything is OK, but, well… Let's say it's only young people who kiss in public—it's not forbidden, but it's not very common.

If you give a gift, you don't have to use both hands. You can use just one hand. There aren't any rules about this sort of thing.

And, no, you don't have to shake hands with everyone when you meet them in Australia. You can shake hands when you meet someone for the first time, in fact, it's bad manners if you don't, but not every time, no.

Lesson 13 Vocabulary and Listening, activity 3

INTERVIEWER Have you always worked here?
ABBY Yes, my father opened the deli the year I was born, in 1922, and I started work when I was fourteen.
INTERVIEWER What about you, Ben?
BEN Well, I started here just after the war, in 1946, so I've been here for fifty-one years.
INTERVIEWER And when did you get married?
ABBY In 1947. It was love at first sight! We just celebrated our golden wedding anniversary.
BEN Yes, we've been married for fifty years. Such a long time…
INTERVIEWER Well, congratulations! Tell me about life in New York.
ABBY I've lived in New York all my life. It's the greatest city in the world!
INTERVIEWER What do you like about it?
ABBY Oh, it's so interesting. There are so many different people, there's Coney Island, and Central Park, and our neighbors are great. Really great. We've lived right here in this neighborhood since we got married.
BEN And there's every kind of food, from all over the world.
INTERVIEWER But what about the crime? Have you ever been robbed?
ABBY Oh yes! But we don't keep much cash here, so…
BEN There are bad people everywhere you go.
INTERVIEWER Have you ever wanted to live somewhere else? To travel around the world?
BEN Why? You can see the world right here! You want to see China? Go to Chinatown! You want to see Italy? Go to Little Italy! It's all here. I haven't been out of New York since the war, and I'm very happy.
ABBY I've always wanted to go to France, though… to Paris. Maybe after we retire…
INTERVIEWER And when will that be?
BEN Retire? Me? Never!
ABBY He always says that.

Lesson 15 Vocabulary, activity 2

Conversation 1
MAN Are you asleep?
WOMAN No, not yet. But I'm very tired.
MAN Did you hear that?
WOMAN Hear what?
MAN That noise.
WOMAN No, I didn't.
MAN I think I'll go see what it is.

Conversation 2
MAN 1 Could you move your car, please?
MAN 2 What?
MAN 1 I said, could you move your car?
MAN 2 Why should I?
MAN 1 Because it's in my way.

Conversation 3
WOMAN Excuse me! Could you tell me how to get to Pike Street?
MAN Pike Street. Well, if I were you, I wouldn't start from here.

Conversation 4
TEACHER Quiet! … I said quiet! Stop shouting, Bob! Sit down, Paul! Get your books out! Will you all be quiet!

Lesson 15 Listening and Speaking, activity 2

PATRICE Hey, here's a survey about how you did at school. Want to do it?
JOEL Mm. Sure.
PATRICE OK, so, did you always work very hard?
JOEL Yeah, I guess so. How about you?
PATRICE Yes, I did, too. I think I worked pretty hard, yeah. Hm, what's next…? Umm…
JOEL Did you always listen carefully to your teachers?
PATRICE No way! Only to the good ones! What about you?
JOEL Well, I think I started to listen to the teachers when they were doing stuff I enjoyed.
PATRICE Yeah, OK, this next one says, did you always behave well?
JOEL Nuh-uh! I was umm, a bit of a hell-raiser!
PATRICE Mm. Well, I think I was pretty well-behaved mostly, so I'd say yes, yeah.
JOEL Good for you! Did you pass your tests easily?
PATRICE Well, it depended on what subject, you know, but mostly they were hard. What about you?
JOEL I didn't pass them that easily, but I worked hard at test time, you know…
PATRICE Yeah, yeah, exactly. What about this one, then? Did you always write slowly and carefully?
JOEL Slowly? Compositions always took a long time to write so I guess I was careful… or maybe just goofing off!
PATRICE Ha ha! I guess I was, I was pretty careful and ah, well yeah, yeah I was pretty thorough.
JOEL And do you think your school days were the best days of your life?
PATRICE Are you kidding? I hated school! What about you?
JOEL Well, I didn't hate it, but it sure wasn't the best time of my life!

Lesson 16 Listening, activity 2

A May I help you?
B Yes, I need a flight to Miami.
A One-way or round-trip?
B Round-trip.
A When do you want to travel? It's cheaper if you spend Sunday night in Miami.
B I'll go on Thursday and come back on Tuesday, then.
A And will that be economy or business class?
B Oh, I'll take economy class, please.
A OK, that's going to be $199.87. How would you like to pay?
B Do you take checks?
A No, ma'am, only credit cards.
B OK, I'll use my American Express card, then. Oh, can you arrange a rental car for me at the airport?
A Yes, of course. We can get you a small car for $34.50 a day.
B Perfect! For five days then.
A So, that'll be $327.37 total.
B Thanks.

Lesson 17 Vocabulary and Listening, activity 4

FORECASTER And here's the weather forecast for the world's major cities. Athens, cloudy and 54°. Bangkok, cloudy and 86°. Cairo, sunny and 61°. Geneva, cloudy and 50°. Hong Kong, cloudy and 68°. Istanbul, rainy and 44°. Kuala Lumpur, sunny and 95°. Lisbon, cloudy and 52°. Madrid, rainy and 44°. Moscow, snowy and 14°. New York, sunny and 32°. Paris, snowy and 21°. Prague, sunny and 28°. Rio, cloudy and 20°. Rome, rainy and 48°. Tokyo, snowy and 24°, and finally Warsaw, cloudy and 17°.

Lesson 18 Listening, activity 1

FRANK So, Sally, want to try this quiz? OK, number one, coffee is grown in a, Brazil, b, Canada, c, Sweden. What do you think?
SALLY Brazil! That's easy!
FRANK I think so, yeah, that's, a.
SALLY OK, number two, Daewoo cars are made in Switzerland, Thailand, or Korea?
FRANK Korea, definitely.

SALLY Yeah? OK, so that's, c.

FRANK Number three, Sony computers are made in Japan, the U.S.A., or Germany?

SALLY Japan.

FRANK Mm… a, then.

SALLY OK, umm, number four. Tea is grown in a, India, b, France, or c, England?

FRANK I think it has to be India, right? Don't you think?

SALLY Yeah, definitely, so that's, a for that one.

FRANK OK, number five, tobacco, where's tobacco grown then, Norway, Iceland, or the U.S.A.? Well it's too cold for Iceland.

SALLY Yeah, it's the U.S.A.

FRANK The U.S.A., that's right, so it's c.

SALLY OK, Benetton clothes are made in Italy, France, or Malaysia?

FRANK Benetton, I think that's Italy, don't you?

SALLY Yeah, I think it is. Yeah.

SALLY Er, number seven, Roquefort cheese is made in a, Germany, b, Thailand, or c, France? It's not Germany, is it?

FRANK No, I don't think it's Germany, I think Roquefort is France.

SALLY Yeah, France, OK.

FRANK Right, number eight. The atom bomb was invented by the Japanese, the Americans, or the Chinese?

SALLY The Americans.

FRANK Yeah, the Americans, b.

SALLY Ah, Guernica was painted by Picasso, Turner, or Monet?

FRANK I have absolutely no idea!

SALLY It's by Picasso, I think.

FRANK Picasso, huh? So that's a.

SALLY Right, the Caribbean islands were discovered by Neil Armstrong, Christopher Columbus, or Marco Polo?

FRANK I think that's Christopher Columbus.

SALLY Was it? Are you sure it wasn't Neil Armstrong?

FRANK Yeah, pretty sure.

SALLY OK, that's b.

FRANK OK, telephone, who invented the telephone, Bell, Marconi, or Baird? Baird invented the television, I think.

SALLY Oh, it's Bell.

FRANK Bell?

SALLY Yeah, definitely.

FRANK OK, twelve, *Romeo and Juliet*, who wrote *Romeo and Juliet*? That's simple, isn't it?

SALLY Yeah.

FRANK Go on, then.

SALLY Well, it wasn't Ibsen.

FRANK No, it has to be Shakespeare.

SALLY Yeah, and it wasn't Stephen King!

FRANK No, that's, b, OK.

SALLY Number thirteen. The Blue Mosque in Istanbul was built for a, Sultan Ahmet, b, Ataturk, or c, Suleyman the Magnificent?

FRANK Jeez, I have no idea!

SALLY Me, either. Make a guess!

FRANK OK, I'll say it was Ataturk.

SALLY OK, that's, b then.

FRANK *Yesterday*, right who composed *Yesterday*, Paul McCartney, John Lennon, well, it definitely wasn't Mick Jagger.

SALLY No.

FRANK So Paul McCartney or John Lennon? I think I know.

SALLY I think it's, a, Paul McCartney.

FRANK Mm. I think so, too. And finally, the pyramids, who were they built by, the Pharaohs, the Sultans, or Walt Disney?

SALLY Well, not Walt Disney!

FRANK No, I don't think so!

SALLY It was the Pharaohs wasn't it? Yeah, that's, a.

Lesson 19 **Listening and Reading, activity 2**

CHRIS Good afternoon.

RECEPTIONIST Hi there! Can I help you?

CHRIS Do you have any beds for tonight?

RECEPTIONIST Yes, I think so. You see, I just started work at the hostel. How long would you like to stay?

CHRIS We'll stay for just one night.

RECEPTIONIST Yes, that's OK.

TONY Great!

RECEPTIONIST How old are you?

TONY We're both sixteen.

RECEPTIONIST OK, that'll be $13 each.

CHRIS Is it far from the hostel to Eureka?

RECEPTIONIST No, not really, it's two miles. It takes about an hour on foot.

TONY Is there a bus?

RECEPTIONIST I think so. It takes about fifteen minutes. There's a bus every hour.

TONY What time is the last bus from Eureka?

RECEPTIONIST I think it leaves at nine o'clock. There's not much to do at night.

CHRIS We're exhausted! We need to go to bed early. What time does the hostel close in the morning?

RECEPTIONIST Umm, at eleven A.M. Where are you walking to?

CHRIS We're going to Crescent City. Are you serving dinner tonight?

RECEPTIONIST Yes, we're serving dinner until eight o'clock. And breakfast starts at seven thirty.

TONY And where's the nearest campsite?

RECEPTIONIST I'm not sure. I think it's Fortuna, which is about ten miles north of here. I started work last Monday so I'm very new here.

Lesson 19 **Listening and Reading, activity 4**

CHRIS It's very strange. She said one night cost $13, but it costs $12.

TONY Yes, and she said it was two miles to Eureka.

CHRIS But, in fact, it's three miles.

TONY And she said the last bus left at nine o'clock. But it leaves at eight o'clock.

Lesson 19 **Grammar, activity 3**

CHRIS And she said the bus took fifteen minutes. But in fact, it takes ten minutes.

TONY And she said the hostel closed at eleven A.M., but it's open all day.

CHRIS The brochure says that they serve dinner from six to seven.

TONY But she said they were serving until eight o'clock. And she also said breakfast started at seven thirty…

CHRIS … when, in fact, it says here that breakfast starts at seven.

TONY And she said that Fortuna was ten miles away, but it isn't. It's eight miles away.

CHRIS And she said that Fortuna was north of here. But it's south of here!

Lesson 20 **Reading and Listening, activity 6**

Ruth's Parents

The next afternoon, Jan went over to Ruth's house for tea.

"How do you do, Mr. and Mrs. Clark," Jan said.

"Sit down, Jan," said Mrs. Clark. "Would you like a cup of coffee?"

"Yes, please," said Jan. He didn't feel very comfortable.

Jan stayed for about an hour. Mr. Clark spoke English very quickly and Jan did not always understand.

Outside the door, Jan said to Ruth, "Your parents don't like me very much."

"Don't be silly, Jan," said Ruth. "My parents haven't met many foreigners. It's all right."

"OK, Ruth," said Jan. "I'll see you tomorrow." And he walked away. But he felt unhappy.

Later that evening Ruth asked, "Well, Mom, did you like Jan?"

Ruth's mother said, "Well, he didn't speak English very well. Your father and I liked Bill. What's wrong with an American boyfriend? And Jan is going back to Poland soon."

"But I don't like Bill any more," shouted Ruth and ran out of the room. "I don't like Bill," she said to herself, "but I do like Jan. Maybe I love him."

Macmillan Heinemann English Language Teaching
Between Towns Road, Oxford OX4 3PP, UK
A division of Macmillan Publishers Limited
Companies and representatives throughout the world

ISBN 0 435 29871 2

Text © Simon Greenall 1997
First published 1997
Design and illustration © Macmillan Publishers Limited 1998

Heinemann is a registered trademark of Reed Educational & Professional Publishing Limited

Designed by Newton Harris
Series design by Stafford & Stafford
Cover design by Stafford & Stafford

Illustrations by:

Ivan Allen, pp. 46 (b), 52; Kathy Baxendale, p. 40; Sarah McDonald, pp. 46 (t); Tracy Rich, p. 44; Martin Sanders, pp. 10, 12, 16 (t), 25, 28, 32, 36, 39, 42, 43, 49, 50; Simon Smith, pp. 11, 13, 16 (b), 37.

Commissioned photography by:
Chris Honeywell pp. 2 (br), 14.

Author's Acknowledgments

I am very grateful to all the people who have contributed towards the creation of this book. My thanks are due to:

– All the teachers I have had the privilege to meet on seminars in many different countries and the various people who have influenced my work.

– Paul Ruben for producing the tapes, and the actors for their voices.

– The various schools who piloted the material.

– Simon Stafford for his skilful design.

– James Hunter and Bridget Green for their careful attention to detail and their creative contribution.

– Angela Reckitt for her careful management of the project.

– Jessica Rackham for her extremely thorough and efficient editorial input.

– And last, but by no means least, Jill, Jack and Alex.

Acknowledgments

The author and publisher would like to thank the following for their kind permission to reproduce copyright material in this book:

Heinemann Educational, a division of Reed Educational & Professsional Publishing Limited, for an extract from *Dear Ruth... Love Jan* by N. McIver; Times Publishing Group, Singapore, for an extract from *Culture Shock! USA* by Esther Wanning, published by Times Editions Pte Ltd., Singapore.

The author and publisher would like to thank the following for permission to reproduce their material: Anthony Blake p. 32; British Rail International p. 9; Eye Ubiquitous p. 26 (mr), 31; Hulton Deutsch p. 2 (l); Images pp. 11 (br), 28 (bc), 38; Image Bank pp. 22 (bl), 23 (l), 30, 34 (fl), 40 (b); Pictor pp. 19, 53 (bc); Superstock pp. 28 (tr), 53 (cr); Tony Stone Images pp. 8, 21, 23 (r), 26 (t), 34 (fr), 40 (t), 41, 53 (tl, ml, bl, br); Trip pp. 26 (bl, ml); Zefa pp. 4 (bc), 22 (tr), 34 (ml, mr), 53 (tc, mc).

The publisher would also like to thank: Celia Bingham, British Rail International, Charles Leveroni, Sarah McDonald, Jason Mann, Anthony Reckitt, Marta and Rebecca Stafford, and Chris Winter.

While every effort has been made to locate the owners of copyright, in some cases this has been unsuccessful. We should be grateful to hear from anyone who recognises their copyright material and who is unacknowledged. We shall be pleased to make the necessary amendments in future editions of the book.

Printed in China

2003 2002 2001 2000
11 10 9 8 7 6 5